APPLICATIONS OF NEURO-LINGUISTIC PROGRAMMING

BY
ROBERT B. DILTS
© DILTS STRATEGY GROUP

Dilts Strategy Group
P.O. Box 67448
Scotts Valley, California 95067
Phone: +1 (831) 438-8314
E-Mail: info@diltsstrategygroup.com
Homepage: http://www.diltsstrategygroup.com

©Copyright 1983 by Robert B. Dilts and Dilts Strategy Group. All rights reserved. This book or parts thereof may not be reproduced in any form without written permission of the Publisher.

Library of Congress Card Number 83-061049
I.S.B.N. 978-1-947629-25-7
I.S.B.N. 13: 978-0-916990-13-8
I.S.B.N. 10: 0-916990-13-3

TABLE OF CONTENTS

I. Applications of Neuro-Linguistic Programming to Business Communication

II. Applications of Neuro-Linguistic Programming in Sales

III. Applications of Neuro-Linguistic Programming in Family Therapy and Interpersonal Negotiation

IV. The Meta Model Live

V. Application of the Meta Model to the Socratic Method of Philosophical Inquiry

VI. Applications of Neuro-Linguistic Programming in Education

VII. Application of Neuro-Linguistic Programming to Creative Writing

VIII. Applications of NLP in Health

IX. Glossary of NLP Terminology

APPLICATIONS OF NEURO-LINGUISTIC PROGRAMMING TO BUSINESS COMMUNICATION

(1981)

BY

ROBERT B. DILTS AND MARY P. DILTS

TABLE OF CONTENTS

Part	Page
Synopsis	1
I. INTRODUCTION	2
II. NEURO-LINGUISTIC PROGRAMMING	2
A. *History of NLP*	3
B. *Principles behind NLP*	4
III. REPRESENTATIONAL SYSTEMS	5
A. *How They Work*	5
B. *Identifying Them*	6
1. Accessing Cues	6
2. Predicates	8
IV. APPLICATION OF NLP TO BUSINESS COMMUNICATION	9
A. *Uses of NLP in Business*	9
B. *NLP Techniques*	10
1. Pacing	10
2. Translating	13
3. Representational Strategies	15
4. Utilization of Strategies	18
5. Modelling and Installation	19
V. SUMMARY	19
Bibliography	20

SYNOPSIS

Neuro-Linguistic Programming is a model of communication that focuses on identifying and using patterns in the thought processes that influence people's verbal and non-verbal behavior as a means of improving the quality and effectiveness of their communication.

NLP was originally developed by Richard Bandler and John Grinder ten years ago for therapeutic communication, and is now internationally popular in many fields (including business, law, and education). A basic principle behind NLP is that "the map is not the territory," because people experience the world differently by receiving information through the senses or "representational systems." That human beings display exactly how they are receiving information is another NLP principle; and by recognizing this, one can vary one's own communication techniques to match the other person's.

Due to environmental and personal influences, many people develop one representational system more than the rest. Watching eye movement is a means of telling which representational system is being used at a particular time, and listening for predicates (process words) can indicate which representational system is valued the most in the thinking process.

Once it is established how a person is thinking, one

can adapt one's own language to create rapport. It is at this point that NLP is most beneficial to business communication for negotiation purposes. By referring to the same representational system, both individuals or parties will have clearer, more effective communication. This can be accomplished by two NLP techniques—pacing and translating. Pacing involves feeding back the vocabulary of the most valued representational system to the individual, while translating is the rephrasing of words from one representational system to another in a group situation.

I. Introduction

We will begin by providing some background information about NLP, and define the basic principles behind this model of communication. We will then look more specifically at the principles involving representational systems—showing how they can be used and identified. Finally, the application of NLP to communication in business will be covered, using transcripts of dialogue as examples of the techniques involved.

II. NEURO-LINGUISTIC PROGRAMMING

Neuro-Linguistic Programming (NLP) is a model of communication that is presently used internationally. Focusing on thought processes, NLP has found patterns that influence people's verbal and non-verbal behavior. By identifying and using these patterns, NLP practitioners can improve the quality and effectiveness of their communication.

A. History of NLP

The concept for NLP was originated ten years ago by John Grinder and Richard Bandler. These two men studied the working processes of noted therapists such as Fritz Perls (Gestalt), Virginia Satir (family therapy), and Milton H. Erickson, M.D. (medical hypnosis). They also combined their own skills from three disciplines—linguistics, computers, and Gestalt Psychology. As a result, they came up with a behavioral model and a set of operational procedures. As NLP has expanded it has incorporated material from several additional disciplines including cybernetics, philosophy, and neurology. It is also applied in numerous fields, such as law, business, and education. NLP has been offered to the public in the form of training and consulting for the past five years, and seminars on NLP are given internationally. NLP principles are also currently being applied in many areas of computer software design.

The purpose of NLP is to help people, groups, and organizations by working directly with the perceptual maps they have for organizing their experience—particularly those involving decision-making, creativity, learning, and motivation. The name, Neuro-Linguistic Programming, refers to the common process all human beings use for encoding, transferring, and modifying behavior. However, the name can be defined even more specifically:

> "Neuro" (derived from the Greek "neuron" for nerve) stands for the fundamental tenet that all behavior is the result of neurological processes. "Linguistic" (derived from the Latin "lingua" for language) indicates that neural processes are represented, ordered and sequenced into models and strate-

gies through language and communication systems. "Programming" refers to the process of organizing the components of a system (sensory representations) to achieve specific outcomes.[1]

B. Principles behind NLP

"The map is not the territory" is an important and basic principle behind Neuro-Linguistic Programming. People experience the world differently because each person develops his own map or model of the world from the information he receives through his senses, or "representational systems" (sight, sound, feeling, taste, and smell). NLP strives for insight into the many ways people experience the world, taking statements such as 'seeing eye-to-eye' as literal communication about their model of the world.

Another NLP principle is that human beings display how they are thinking in various subtle ways. It is possible for one to recognize signs of thought in another person and detect particular patterns. For instance, the eyes indicate how people are thinking—whether they are visualizing, hearing sounds or words, or feeling. Once the thought process is discovered, one can vary one's own communication techniques to match the other person's and, therefore, establish easy rapport.

NLP also operates by the principle that how one presents one's communication or information will greatly affect how it is perceived by the other person. And the more flexible one is in one's map and presentational style of behavior, the more effective a professional communicator one will be.

[1] Robert Dilts, John Grinder, Richard Bandler et al, *Neuro-Linguistic Programming: Volume I* (California: Meta Publications, 1980), p. 2.

III. Representational Systems

NLP says that all of an individual's ongoing experience must be comprised of some combination of each of his senses or "representational systems." Each person uses his auditory, visual, kinesthetic, and olfactory/gustatory senses to create his model of the world.

A. How They Work

Due to the influences in the personal backgrounds of individuals and the environments in which they develop their representational systems, there is a tendency for many people to develop or value the information processing capabilities of one of their representational systems to a greater degree than others. An auditorally oriented person is one who prefers his ears in perception and who depends on spoken words for the information which is decisive in behavior. A visually oriented person primarily uses his eyes to perceive the world around him, and uses visual images in remembering and in thinking. A kinesthetically oriented person is one who feels his way through his experiences; both external and internal stimuli are sorted through the feelings and these feelings determine his decisions. (According to NLP, olfaction and gustation are not primary senses, especially in this culture, and so they will not be focused on in the following discussions and examples; however, this would include those who perceive the world through tastes or smells, such as cooks.) The predominant representational system will usually come out most obviously when a person is in a stressful state.

If a particular representational system is valued

or developed more than the others, it can be either an asset or a limitation, depending on the flexibility one has in approaching or developing the others. Nevertheless, the representational system that is most highly valued will always greatly affect the way that person perceives and acts upon the world.

B. Identifying Them

1. Accessing Cues

NLP maintains that the eyes are more than just a "window to the soul." Through clinical and experimental research, NLP has found that the direction and position to which an individual momentarily averts his eyes, when recalling information or answering a question, correspond to the representational system he is accessing. During interaction, when a person often breaks eye contact, the eye movements indicate whether one is using pictures, words, or feelings in thinking and remembering. These eye movements are a class of behavior called "accessing cues." In the following diagram, the directions of the eyes are explained according to which representational system is used:

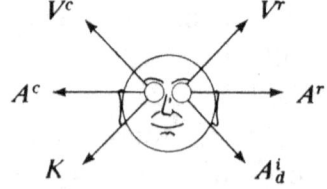

Accessing Cues

Applications of NLP to Business Communication

V^c Visual constructed images
[visualizing something never seen before]

V^r Visual remembered images
[visualizing something seen before]

(Eyes defocused and unmoving also indicate visual accessing.)

A^c Auditory constructed sounds or words
[hearing sounds or words never heard before]

A^r Auditory remembered sounds or words
[remembering sounds or conversations from the past]

K Kinesthetic feelings (also smell and taste)
[sensing inner, past feelings and imagining future ones]

A^i_d Auditory sounds or words
[indicates talking to self]

The best way to support this finding is to try it on someone. Using the diagram for reference, and a few questions, one should be able to "see" the person put to use the different representational systems. The questions to ask must be about some small detail that the person wouldn't have memorized, but would have to think about. A sample visual question would be: What color is your toothbrush? An auditory question would have to be about a familiar sound that one does not need to picture, such as: How many times do you hear the word "lamb" in the nursery rhyme, "Mary Had a Little Lamb?" To get a kinesthetic reaction, one would have to ask a question like: Do you breathe more deeply when you feel excited or when you feel surprised? Some questions can be answered using any system, so one would need to be careful in choosing questions to test the accuracy of accessing cues.

2. Predicates

While noting how a person gathers information, NLP says that one can also look for that person's means of understanding what he gathers by listening to the words he selects. Of the three senses primarily used by most people—seeing, hearing, feeling—one is often preferred by an individual over the other two for perceiving stimuli and storing them, for making decisions, and for organizing their experience. This preferred sense can be identified by the predicates—adjectives, adverbs, verbs, and any other descriptive language—used in the speech. NLP considers there to be a revealing tendency for people to do what they are talking about. Through their language, people will literally tell you which representational system they are employing to make sense of and organize their ongoing experience. In the following word groupings, examples of predicates are provided for each of the three senses:

Predicates Used by the Visual, the Auditory, and the Kinesthetic

Visual: I *see* what you are saying; that doesn't *look* quite right; I need to get *clear* on this idea; it's sort of *hazy* right now; I just go *blank;* that casts some *light* on the subject; we need a new *perspective;* a *colorful* example.

Auditory: That *rings a bell;* I *hear* you; it *sounds* good to me; *listen* to this; it just suddenly *clicked; tune* in to what they're trying to *say;* I had to *ask* myself; that

	idea has been *rattling* around in my head for a while.
Kinesthetic:	I've got a good *feeling* about this project; get a *handle* on this; he needs to get in *touch* with the *flow* of the sentiment; a *solid* proposal; we're *up against a wall;* that's a *heavy* problem; can you *grasp* what needs to be done?

IV. Application of NLP to Business Communication

When applied to communication in business, NLP is used primarily for negotiation purposes.

A. Uses of NLP in Business

The ability of business people to observe and diagnose the representational systems of the individuals they are working with can be invaluable in attaining goals with those individuals. These goals can include the negotiation of some decision, the building of a team, or even a sale.

For instance, in a decision-making situation, mis-communication can occur when different parties (or individuals) are referring to different representational systems, thus talking right past each other. However, if both are referring to the same representational system, communication can be quickly understandable and clear. In a selling situation, a salesman can learn to detect not only word signals but other signs of how a buyer is thinking (the most obvious being eye movement), and then use language that reflects the buyer's mode of perception.

A book on how to clarify language in business situations has been organized specifically for businessmen and women. It is called *Precision*, by John Grinder and Michael McMaster, and is useful in communication, sales, meetings, negotiation, and organization.

B. NLP Techniques

Once it is discovered *how* people are thinking—by watching for accessing cues and/or listening for predicates—one can adapt one's own language to harmonize with them by appealing to their perceptual manner. This can be accomplished by two techniques—pacing and translating.

1. Pacing

The most effective way to apply the information gathered about the representational systems when working with an individual is to use "pacing." Pacing is the process of using and feeding back the most valued representational system of the other person, or going to his model of the world. It involves having the flexibility to pick up and incorporate the individual's vocabulary into one's own vocabulary. The process is important to all of the essential aspects of good business communication, (such as rapport and trust building), and it can help in organizing the kind of interventions one desires.

Sample conversations are probably the best way to clarify how this process works. The following transcripts of dialogue illustrate the function of pacing. The first transcript establishes how mis-communication occurs due to the lack of pacing between a "visual" and a "kinesthetic:"

Visual: If you look over that proposal again you would see clearly that I've focused on all of the important issues. I don't see what's bothering you.

Kinesthetic: I just keep getting the feeling that something is missing. I can't put my finger on it, but there is something we need to get a better handle on.

Visual: I think you are stuck in your own point of view. If you looked at it from my perspective you would be able to see how this is going to work.

Kinesthetic: I don't think you're getting in touch with the solid issues, and there could be some heavy problems if you don't come to grips with those.

It is apparent that these two people are talking right past each other—one using words that refer to what he sees, the other using words about how he feels. The next transcript exemplifies mis-communication between a "visual" and an "auditory:"

Auditory: I want to talk with you because I've had some ideas rattling around in my head and I would like to find out how they sound to you.

Visual: Let me look at what you've got. Do you have them drawn up anywhere? What can you show me?

Auditory: Well, they are something I've just started to tune in to, and I wanted to use you as a sounding board. It's nothing to shout about, but I thought maybe we could play it by ear.

Visual: When you have something definite to show me then come back in. Once I can see that you have something worthwhile to look at, then we can focus on it.

Once again mis-communication has occurred because neither person will recognize the representational system to which the other refers. This next transcript provides an example of pacing for each representational system:

Visual: As I look back over this proposal you showed me, I think there are some grey areas in it. I am not clear about what you were trying to say all along.

Pace: I think I can see what you are saying. Let me try to paint a picture of it so that I can illustrate my ideas a bit better. Then I am sure we will see eye-to-eye on it.

Auditory: I think we need to talk about this some more. I've listened to what you have had to say and it sounds like there might be some discord between what you're saying and I'm thinking.

Pace: I think I can tune into what you're saying. I hear you. Let's replay our conversation for a minute and talk about what might be missing. Then maybe I can resonate with you on this.

Kinesthetic: I can't seem to get in touch with what you're saying. I feel as though you might just be spinning your wheels on this. I just can't get a handle on the meat of your proposal.

Pace: I think I can connect with you on that. I don't want to put you over a barrel on this, and my back is up against the wall, too. I'd like to take a little of the weight off, so let's walk back through the proposal and we'll try to find any soft spots.

Thus, by feeding back words that acknowledge and reflect the representational system used by the individual, communication and agreement can occur more rapidly and with greater ease.

2. Translating

"Translating" is the rephrasing of words from one representational system to another. It involves matching and mis-matching predicates so that a "visual" begins to understand the world of a "kinesthetic," or an "auditory" that of a "visual." This technique especially applies to group negotiations.

As before, a transcript of dialogue will be used to illustrate how the technique works. In this example, mis-communication has occurred between Barbara (a "visual") and Bill (a "kinesthetic"). The

NLP negotiator is translating the ideas using typical predicates to appeal to the different representational systems:

Barbara: He keeps showing me this proposal but it looks so messy and scattered. I don't see how anything that looks this disorganized can improve our image with the public.

Bill: I think that she is insensitive to the things that are really important to people. This proposal expresses the way a lot of people feel. If she wasn't so numb to people's feelings, she would be able to get in touch with how this can work.

Negotiator: Barbara, I think that what Bill is trying to say is that you need to shift your perspective about this proposal, and look past the details so that you can focus on the big picture. Then you'll see that there are certain issues that are going to stand out more clearly than others.

Bill, I think you've got to put yourself in Barbara's shoes. When she tries to connect with this the way it is presented, I think she feels that she is being pulled in all different directions, and there is nothing she feels she can hold on to. Keep the proposal grounded and steady. Instead of rubbing her the wrong way, I think it would help things fall together more smoothly.

The NLP negotiator acts literally as a translator, transferring the messages by using words that refer to the different representational systems.

3. Representational Strategies

People are not always in only one representational system or another.

As we carry out various tasks and achieve various outcomes through our behavior we must focus in on different representational systems at different points in time. For instance, each of you readers as you read this sentence has a strategy for taking these particular patterns of black ink on the white page and making meaning out of it for yourself. As you read these words you must first focus your attention to external visual (V^e) experience to see the words written before you. You then turn your attention inward to make sense of the images that your eye reports. You may be hearing your own voice in your head (A^i) saying each word that you see. Perhaps you are making an internal visual image (V^i) of yourself as you read, or of the information on the previous page. Or perhaps these visual patterns have accessed in you some feelings of interest or recognition (K^i).

Certain kinds of strategies are more effective for achieving outcomes in certain tasks but may be inefficient for others. The task of taking a chemistry test for example is most effectively achieved by a strategy involving internal visual and auditory recall of formulas and diagrams. This would be a very inefficient strategy to apply to the task of playing basketball, however, which requires much greater attention to external visual and kinesthetic experience.

Those of you readers who have an effective strategy for achieving the outcome of reading rapidly, or speed reading, will probably be aware that for the most part you do not repeat the words that you see before you in your head to yourself but move directly to other forms of internal experience by which you make sense of the written words. The information that you get by repeating the words to yourself is in one sense redundant since you have already gathered the information by looking at the words, and the process of saying each word to yourself adds in another step that takes much longer than if you were only to scan the words visually.

One important aspect of considering behavior in terms of strategies is that one quickly realizes that it is the form of the processing strategy that determines most of the efficiency and effectiveness that one has with a particular task, rather than the amount of time one has spent doing the task. For instance, you may have been reading for over forty years and have read thousands of books, but if your strategy for reading is such that you say the words to yourself in your head you may be a slower and less efficient reader than someone who has only a fraction of the experience that you have had with reading, but has a more streamlined strategy.

The same is true for the tasks involved in being a good manager, supervisor, executive, engineer, etc. It is the strategy that you use to make sense of the situations that are offered to you that determines your effectiveness at the task. A manager who continually responds to the images in his head of how things are "supposed" to look may not be able to pick up and respond to important visual cues that are in his immediate sensory environment.

The well-known "Peter principle," in fact, is the

Applications of NLP to Business Communication

result of the fact that many individuals, who have or are able to develop a very effective strategy for one set of tasks, do not have the flexibility in behavior to be able to adapt their strategies to a new set of tasks that are presented to them when they are promoted.

It is common for individuals to develop a most highly valued strategy sequence through which they process practically all of their experience. A person, for example, may have a decision strategy that initially involves his asking questions (A^e). In answer to these questions the person is shown (V^e) or visualizes (V^i) a series of possible solutions. The person then gets a feeling (K^i) about each of these images and chooses the one that feels the best. We can notate the representational sequence involved in this strategy in the following way:

$$A^e \rightarrow V^e \text{ or } V^i \rightarrow K^i \rightarrow \text{DECISION}.$$

Some individuals may go through this same sequence whether they are deciding what kind of car to buy, what to eat on a menu, which proposal to accept or whom to vote for for president.

As we pointed out earlier, developing or valuing a particular representational strategy sequence to a greater degree than the others can be either an asset or a limitation, depending on the flexibility you have in accessing or developing others.

The ability of the businessperson or consultant to observe and determine the representational strategies of the individuals he is working with can be one of the most critical factors of his professional success.

4. Utilization of Strategies

One of the most effective ways of applying the information you have gathered about representational strategies when you are working with individuals or groups is to *pace* their strategies. A person can't not respond to his own processes for organizing his experience—it is therefore generally much quicker to work through the processes that he has developed for himself rather than try to impose your own on him.

Pacing involves the ability of the communicator to have the flexibility to be able to pick up and incorporate the vocabulary and non-verbal communication of an individual or group, and to be able to translate his ideas into that vocabulary. It also involves the ability of the communicator to package his information in a form and sequence that is most compatible with the processing strategies of the client. For example, packaging your information in a form most compatible with the decision strategy of the individual we mentioned earlier, whose sequence went:

$$A^e \rightarrow V^e \text{ or } V^i \rightarrow K^i \rightarrow \text{DECISION},$$

might involve a presentation like, "I'm sure you have a lot of questions to ask (A^e) about this project, and as you can see (V^e) I've been asking a lot of questions myself (A^e) and have really looked hard (V^e or V^i) for the answers . . . And I believe I can show you (V^e) the solution that I'm sure you will feel (K^i) is the most solid (K^i) way to proceed."

Because the presentation fits the natural progression of the individual's strategy it will be much easier for that individual to follow and, because it paces the individual's own decision strategy, it can often become irresistible to the person.

In team building, for instance, you will want to utilize the information you have gathered about your participants' strategies to engineer the appropriate kind and sequence of interactions that will take place between the task team members.

5. Modelling and Installation

Another powerful application of the information gathering tools provided by the NLP model is that of extracting and modelling the strategies of individuals who are able to perform some task extremely well, and then teaching this strategy to someone else. This, in a sense, allows the NLP practitioner to "clone" behavior. By knowing the specific representational sequence an individual employs in effectively achieving outcomes for a particular task, this sequence may be installed into the behavior of another individual to obtain the same behavioral abilities.

The modelling and installation process is discussed in depth in *Neuro-Linguistic Programming Vol I.*

V. Summary

Neuro-Linguistic Programming is a rapidly developing model of communication that appeals to a wide variety of people in many professions all over the world. In business, NLP is used mostly by managers and salespeople for negotiation purposes. In such situations, the NLP process involves identifying the preferred representational system and strategies of an individual by watching eye movement and listening to predicates. These indicate how that individual gathers and understands information. The next step applies the technique of either pacing or translating—using pacing for one-to-one negotiations and translating for group negotiations. This step makes sure that the communicants are referring to the same representational system or strategy. The result is clearer, more effective communication that helps to establish understanding quickly and to attain goals.

Bibliography

Bandler, Richard, and Grinder, John *Frogs into Princes,* Real People Press, Utah, 1979, 194 pp.

_____, *Patterns of the Hypnotic Techniques of Milton H. Erickson, M.D. I,* Meta Publications, California, 1975, 265 pp.

Dilts, Robert, Grinder, John and Bandler, Richard *Neuro-Linguistic Programming: Volume I,* Meta Publications, California, 1980, 284 pp.

Dilts, Robert, "Neuro-Linguistic Programming in Organizational Development," *Conference Presentation Papers,* New York, 1979, pp. 4–11.

Laborde, Genie, "Neuro-Linguistic Programming," *New Realities,* Vol. IV 1981, pp. 8–14.

Maron, Davida, "Neuro-Linguistic Programming: The Answer to Change," *Training and Development Journal* 1979, pp. 68–71.

APPLICATIONS OF NEURO-LINGUISTIC PROGRAMMING IN SALES

(1982)

BY

ROBERT B. DILTS

TABLE OF CONTENTS

PART	PAGE
I. INTRODUCTION	3
A. The Three Qualities of a Professional Communicator	4
II. SETTING OUTCOMES	4
A. Rapport	7
B. State Outcomes in Positive Terms	8
III. SENSORY EXPERIENCE	8
A. Calibration	10
IV. BEHAVIORAL FLEXIBILITY	11
A. Principles of Flexibility	14

I. INTRODUCTION

Have you ever wondered what, specifically, top salespeople do to consistently and elegantly please their customers and close sales?

Good sales skills are one of the most important elements of success for any professional communicator.

A professional communicator is someone who makes a living from his or her communications with other people. Salespeople, managers, educators, trainers, psychotherapists, lawyers and many others all fall under this title. Some professional communicators sell products directly; others must sell themselves and their ideas.

Neuro-Linguistic Programming (NLP) is a model of behavior and communication that provides a framework and a set of skills and operational procedures that can allow anyone to achieve the successful results of top salespeople. Neuro-Linguistic Programming, as the name implies, is a model about how our brains work (Neuro); about how language interacts with the brain (Linguistic); and about how to use what we know about these to systematically get the results we want for ourselves and our clients (Programming).

By modelling the behavior of people at the top of their professions we can furnish our own models of the world with specific skills and techniques which have made others especially effective.

A. The Three Qualities of a Professional Communicator

From our observations of professional communicators in many different fields we have found that there are three qualities that are universal to every successful communicator:

(1) Good communicators continually set explicit and verifiable outcomes or goals.

(2) Good communicators have the sensory awareness and observational skill to provide them with feedback about their progress toward their outcomes.

(3) Good communicators have flexibility of behavior and continually change and adjust their communication to achieve their outcomes. If one approach isn't working they have the flexibility to easily switch to another.

It is these three qualities that the techniques of NLP are designed to instill and develop.

II. Setting Outcomes

When setting outcomes for yourself and other people it is critical to keep in mind that EVERYBODY HAS HIS OR HER OWN MENTAL MAP OF THE WORLD. When a person wants to buy something, communicate something or understand something that person will construct a mental floor plan of the product or outcome that they want. It is the job of the professional communicator to appraise (and in some instances to help develop) the mental floor plan of their client or customer and to provide as many options and choices as they can that will fit that map.

Many salespeople end up (unconsciously) selling themselves a product rather than the customer. They make the mistake of presupposing that the customer thinks the same way that they do.

Consider for a moment which of the following houses would appeal to you the most:

> The first house is quite picturesque. It has a very quaint look to it. You can see that a lot of focus has been put on the colorful patio and garden area. It has a lot of window space so that you can enjoy the view. It is clearly a good buy.

> The second house is very soundly constructed and situated. It is in such a quiet area that all you hear when you walk outside are the sounds of the birds singing. Its storybook interior tells of so much character that you'll probably find yourself asking yourself how you could ever pass it by.

> The third house is not only solidly constructed, it has a real special feel to it as well. It's not often that you come in contact with a place that touches on so many important features. It is spacious enough that you really feel like you can move around freely and yet cozy enough that you won't wear yourself out taking care of it.

Which one did you choose?

Actually, these are all descriptions of the same house! The only difference is that each description was written to appeal to a different sense. If you chose the first house you are probably more visually (sight) oriented. If you chose house number two you are most likely more auditorally (sound) oriented. If you chose the third, you probably value your feelings more than your other senses.

People's maps of the world are constructed from experiences they perceive through their sensory representational systems (sight, hearing, feelings, taste and smell). People will often find themselves more at home with one sense than the others as they build their mental floor plans. For some people "seeing is believing;" others rely much more heavily on their feelings; while others value what they hear and seek the verbal opinions of other people.

Since people are largely unconscious of their own mental processes it is vital to listen to the language of customers and clients. It is not uncommon to find interactions like the following:

CUSTOMER: This house is nice . . . but I want a place that really FEELS like home.

SALESPERSON: Well let's LOOK around some more. There's a nice VIEW out the back window.

C: OK, but I just keep getting the FEELING that something is missing and I can't quite PUT MY FINGER ON what it is.

S: Well maybe if you PICTURE what your furniture would LOOK like in here you would be able to SEE it more as "home."

In this dialogue, the salesperson is trying to please the buyer (who is feelings oriented) but is not in contact with his or her most valued representational system. Stuck in his own most highly valued representational system (visual), the salesperson has no idea that he is on the wrong track for this buyer.

If this salesperson had been trained to use NLP to assess his client's foremost representational system (feelings) he might have responded something like this:

CUSTOMER: This house is nice but . . . I want a place that really FEELS like home.

SALESPERSON: That's an important FEELING for me too. Perhaps you could put me IN TOUCH with what kind of FEELING that is for you.

C. Well, I really need to FEEL that there will be room for a growing family. I hate FEELING CRAMPED.

By pacing the customer's most valued representational system and asking directly about his or her mental floor plan, the salesperson is then able to uncover explicit information about what will give the client the FEELING that he or she wants and no longer has to play hit and miss.

A. Rapport

Of critical importance when you are gathering information from your clients and customers about their needs and goals is the ability to establish RAPPORT with them. The quality of information you get from your clients will directly relate to the amount of rapport you have with them. People generally experience more rapport with people who share the same model of the world that they do. Pacing language patterns is only one way of going to someone else's model of the world. Pacing or subtlely mirroring their non-verbal communication can also greatly enhance their experience of rapport because they will perceive you as being "like them." Some ways to non-verbally pace or mirror a potential client or customer include putting yourself into a similar body posture, using similar intonation patterns and expressions, dressing similarly, etc.

B. STATE OUTCOMES IN POSITIVE TERMS

Another important feature about establishing goals for yourself and others is to make sure that they are STATED IN THE POSITIVE. When you ask people what they want they will often respond by telling you what they don't want. The customer in our example, for instance, stated the desired outcome by describing what she wanted to avoid ("I hate FEELING CRAMPED"). Many salespeople make the mistake of presupposing that they know what "cramped" means. The experienced, successful communicator, on the other hand, would continue the questioning by asking, "What feeling would you have if you didn't feel cramped?" Here the salesperson is asking the client for the feeling he or she DOES want as opposed to what he or she wants to avoid.

III. Sensory Experience

Words are only one of the ways that people communicate. A person's non-verbal communication is as important, if not more so, than their verbal communication. Words typically represent the things that a person is conscious of while most non-verbal behavior is out of awareness. People will offer you a large number of unconscious non-verbal cues that can be used if you train yourself to observe and respond to them.

One important discovery of NLP, for instance, has been that people move their eyes to specific places when they think. NLP provides a specific index for how these eye positions correspond to the representational system people use to view, get in touch with or tune in to their mental floor plan.

Applications of Neuro-Linguistic Programming in Sales

The following listing shows how eye movements and representational systems are related:

EYE POSITION	REPRESENTATIONAL SYSTEM
up and right	constructed pictures
up and left	remembered images
level and right	constructed sounds
level and left	remembered sounds
down and right	feelings
down and left	talking to yourself

These cues will accurately indicate which sensory system a person is using at a point in time. (NOTE: Many left-handed people will be reversed right-to-left with respect to the above chart.)

Taking this observational skill back to our customer/salesperson example, we can use it to gain additional understanding of the buyer's decision strategy. Let us suppose that right before the customer said, "I just keep getting the FEELING that something is missing but I can't quite PUT MY FINGER ON it," she moved her eyes level and to the left. Using the table above, we can predict that she is remembering hearing something. The salesperson may then direct his or her inquiries to be more on target by asking something like, "Well, is there something we still need to TALK about? Are you still concerned that there might be a NOISE problem with the neighbors?"

Again, by using his or her observations of the buyer's eye movements, the salesperson can continue to gather on-target information, even though the client herself is not aware of it.

It should be noted that the NLP observational skills are oriented towards the form of the other person's thinking as opposed to the content. Many sales training courses make the mistake of teaching people to prejudge or make guesses about the content of their customer's thoughts. For instance, they may teach that "when he strokes his chin it means he's ready to buy." In our experience we have found that content-based interpretations of this sort can often be way off the mark and can create misinterpretations that will jeopardize the salesperson's rapport with the client.

In contrast, we have observed that when someone is stroking his/her chin or face (the so-called "telephone postures") it is typically an indication that he or she is talking to him/herself. WHAT he or she is saying, however, is something that cannot be determined ahead of time. This type of determination must be made by carefully pairing the specific non-verbal cues of a specific person with specific statements and responses the salesperson has elicited.

A. CALIBRATION

CALIBRATION is the name, in NLP, given to the process of learning how to read another person's responses in an ongoing interaction. Instead of prejudging or hallucinating about the internal responses of their clients, good communicators learn to read responses in the ongoing situation. For example, let's say that the salesperson in our example had noticed that every time the buyer talked about feeling "cramped" she furrowed her eyebrows, tightened her shoulder muscles and clenched her teeth slightly. If at some time later he observed these same cues as the buyer was looking at a particular room in a house, he would have evidence that she is experiencing the "cramped" response and may respond appropriately to it.

Having the sensory awareness to make these kinds of observations is a critically important skill in all parts of communication. One way to sharpen your skills in this area is to practice this simple exercise. Ask a friend or associate to think of something they were really satisfied with. As they are thinking of it observe their eye movements, facial expression, breathing rate and postural changes. Then ask them to think of something that they were dissatisfied with and carefully observe again. You should be able to see some differences in their non-verbal response to the two thoughts. Finally, ask them to think of one or the other of the two experiences but not to tell you which one it is. Then "read their mind" by seeing which set of cues you observe as they are thinking, and telling them which thought it is. You may be surprised at how accurate you can be.

IV. Behavioral Flexibility

Once an outcome has been established and the relevant sensory cues identified, the success of the communicator will depend on his or her ability to vary his or her behavior so that the impact of that behavior leads toward the outcome—completing the transaction.

A key factor in achieving flexibility in your behavior is the ability to perceive your customer's needs and potential objections as feedback or opportunities rather than as failures or limitations. A good example of this difference in attitude is the story of the two sales representatives of two different shoe companies who were sent to Mexico to try to open up some new markets for their respective companies. After about a month one of the salespeople wired home with the message, "I'm coming back home. Everyone down here wears sandals. There's no market for shoes." At the same time, however, the other sales representative wired his company saying, "Send all the shoes you can get down here! No one's got any. We'll be able to clean up!"

What one person saw as a limitation, the other saw as an opportunity.

Another humorous example of the power of feedback and flexibility is the story of the young grocery clerk. He was very conscientious and hard-working and the boss had his eye on him as a good candidate for a promotion. One day, however, an elderly and extremely cantankerous customer approached the youth as he was in the produce department and rudely demanded that the youth sell him half a head of lettuce. After patiently trying to explain a number of times that the store did not sell lettuce in half heads, the youth became tired of the abuse he was receiving from the old man and said he would need to go ask his boss. Reaching the back of the store, the youth called back to his boss saying, "Hey, some jerk out here wants to buy a half a head of lettuce . . ." Having well developed sensory awareness, however, the youth suddenly noticed in his peripheral vision that the old man had followed him to the back of the store and just heard every word he had said. Applying the flexibility principle, however, the youth turned and with a gallant gesture continued, ". . . and this fine gentleman would like the other half."

After the old man had left, the boss congratulated the young man on his ability to turn a potentially disastrous situation around and said, "You know,

I've had my eye on you for a long time. I was really impressed by the way you handled that incident today. How would you like to be the manager of the new store I'm opening up in Canada?" The youth thought for a moment and said, "I don't know if I'd like it in Canada. I hear all that's up there are whores and hockey players." Suddenly very indignant, the boss growled, "Well, my wife is from Canada!" With an innocent smile the youth naturally asked, "Oh really . . . What team did she play for?"

Applying the flexibility principle to our previous example, let's say that when the salesperson asked, "Is there anything we still need to talk about?" the customer replied, "Well when my husband and I DISCUSSED it we both agreed that we should get a place with a big back yard . . . and this house doesn't have much of a back yard at all." If the salesperson accepts this statement as a limitation he or she will be stuck.

If, on the other hand, he or she were to combine the flexibility principle with outcome orientation he would ask:

SALESPERSON: What do you want a big back yard for?

CUSTOMER: We're planning on raising a family and we want to have plenty of room for the children to play.

SALESPERSON: Oh, so what you really want is a place for the kids to play. Well there is a nice park about two blocks from here. There would be plenty of room for the children . . . and just think of all the money you'd save on property taxes.

Even if the customer had responded instead with something like, "We want a big back yard because we were planning on raising Arabian horses," the salesperson could still employ the flexibility principle and respond:

S: That's interesting. What do you want to raise Arabian horses for?

C: Well, we were thinking about raising them and racing them later as a way to get a little return on our investment.

S: Ah, so you are interested in investments. Well, this house has a lot of potential as an investment . . .

A. PRINCIPLES OF FLEXIBILITY

One of the beliefs that NLP stresses in regard to flexibility in communication is that THERE IS NO SUCH THING AS RESISTANT CLIENTS OR CUSTOMERS, THERE ARE ONLY INFLEXIBLE SALESPEOPLE, MANAGERS, THERAPISTS, ETC. Have you ever tried to talk to someone but found you were not getting through to him or her? If you find a barrier such as this, try another approach. As soon as there is a behavior you can't perform there is a response you can't elicit. Perhaps a more fundamental way to state the principle we want to communicate would be to say that IF WHAT YOU ARE DOING IS NOT GETTING THE OUTCOME YOU WANT THEN DO SOMETHING DIFFERENT. If you have already proved to yourself that what you are doing isn't working then doing anything else is a better option. And although these principles may sound like simple common sense you would be surprised at how many people get stuck doing one or two techniques over and over again because they worked once before.

A final principle to keep in mind when you are establishing outcomes and varying your behavior is that THE MEANING OF YOUR COMMUNICATION IS THE RESPONSE YOU ELICIT, REGARDLESS OF WHAT YOU INTENDED BY THAT COMMUNICATION. Sometimes when a person is trying to be helpful or thoughtful, for instance, the other person may misinterpret it or respond adversely to it. Rather than be angry or hurt in such a situation, DO SOMETHING DIFFERENT. The people we communicate with cannot read our minds. If a client responds with irritation or mistrust then that is the meaning of the communication to that client, and if you want a different response, vary your behavior until you elicit a response that fits your desired outcome.

Our brains provide the blueprints for our behavior. Knowing some simple facts about the brain can give professional communicators exclusive insights into how their clients and customers map their world and thus increase the effectiveness of communication many times over.

APPLICATIONS OF NEURO-LINGUISTIC PROGRAMMING™ IN FAMILY THERAPY AND INTERPERSONAL NEGOTIATION

BY ROBERT DILTS AND JEREMY DAVID GREEN

© META PUBLICATIONS, 1980

TABLE OF CONTENTS

PARTS	PAGE
DEFINITION	3
HISTORICAL DEVELOPMENT	4
PRESUPPOSITIONS OF NLP	6
1. The Map is Not the Territory	6
2. Mind and Body are Part of the Same System and Affect Each Other	9
3. Individual Skills are a function of the Development and Sequencing of Representational Systems	11
4. The Meaning of any Communication is the Response it Elicits, Regardless of the Intent of the Communicator.	14
5. Human Beings are Capable of One Trial Learning	15
6. Individuals Have All the Resources They Need to Achieve Their Desired Outcomes	17
7. Behavior is Geared Toward Adaptation	19
8. There is No Substitution in Communication for Clean, Active, Open Sensory Channels	20

TABLE OF CONTENTS

PART	PAGE
a. The Element in a system that has the Most Flexibility will be the Controlling, or Catalytic, Element in that System.	21
THERAPIST'S ROLE	23
CLIENT'S ROLE	31
Present State: Problems of Clients	34
Desired State: Goals of Therapeutic Process	35
1. The Outcome Must be Stated in Positive Terms	36
2. The Outcome Must be Testable and Demonstrable in Sensory Experience	36
3. The Desired State Must be Initiated and Maintained by the Client	37
4. The Outcome Must be Explicitly and Appropriately Contextualized	38
5. The Desired State Must Preserve Any Positive By-Products of the Present State	39
6. The Desired State Must be Ecologically Sound.	39
TECHNIQUES	40
Anchoring	44
Reframing	49

Establishing A Self-Reinforcing Loop	52
Future Pacing	55
CASE EXAMPLE	57
SUMMARY	63
EVALUATION AND RESEARCH	65
SUGGESTED READINGS	67
AUTHORS	69
REFERENCES	70

DEFINITION

Neuro-Linguistic Programming™ is a discipline that was developed to answer the question, "How, specifically, do individuals at the top of their professions consistently and elegantly achieve their desired outcomes?" In the past decade this question has been applied to great professional communicators in the fields of psychotherapy, business, education, and law by the founders and developers of NLP™. Through this process, the question has evolved to an even more fundamental query, "What is the structure of subjective experience in humans?" The answers to these questions have resulted in the development of a set of powerful, effective, and systematic tools of communication and change, designed to help anyone in a profession that involves face-to-face communication achieve desired outcomes, more efficiently and effectively.

According to Dilts et al. (1980):

> "Neuro" stands for the fundamental tenet that all behavior is the result of neurological processes. "Linguistic" indicates that neural processes are represented, ordered, and sequenced into models and strategies through language and communications systems. "Programming" refers to the process of organizing the components of a system to achieve a specific outcome (p. 2).

Indeed, Neuro-Linguistic Programming™ is an outcome-oriented discipline. The outcome in family therapy is insuring that every member of the family can get desired external behaviors and internal responses from other members of the family without having to give up, or compromise, any of their own personal integrity, or disrupt the ecology of the family system. This chapter will present a few of the tools that we, and our colleagues, have developed to achieve that outcome in the family therapy context. We caution the reader that these tools are only maps, and the "map is not the territory." The maps are not substitutes for the ability to set a trajectory toward an outcome, or the ability to use what you see, hear, or feel as feedback about your position on that trajectory, or the ability to be flexible in your behavior (inside or outside the maps by which you operate) to achieve that outcome.

HISTORICAL DEVELOPMENT

Neuro-Linguistic Programming had its origins in the early 1970s at the University of California at Santa Cruz where Richard Bandler and John Grinder began to develop a linguistic model for the therapeutic process. Bandler, a mathematician, and Grinder, a linguist, became curious about how language could produce change in people. They modeled the linguistic patterns that Virginia Satir, Fritz Perls, and they themselves used in therapy contexts that produced successful outcomes for clients. The result of this modeling of the model of language in therapy was the development of the meta model. The meta model provides the therapist with an explicit set of questions and questioning techniques to both reconnect the client with his model of the world and to assist the therapist in understanding the client's model of the world. The meta model in published form became *The Structure of Magic, Volume I.*

During the publication process of *The Structure of Magic,* Gregory Bateson told Bandler and Grinder about the work of Milton Erickson, a therapeutic genius who was considered to be the foremost practitioner of medical hypnosis in the world. They traveled to Phoenix, Arizona to study with Erickson and discovered that, indeed, he was a genius at the art of therapy and hypnosis. Their modeling of the linguistic and behavioral patterns in Erickson's hypnotic and therapeutic work with clients became *The Patterns of the Hypnotic Techniques of Milton H. Erickson, M.D., Volume I,* and *Patterns II,* co-authored with Judith DeLozier.

After modeling Erickson, Bandler and Grinder continued their modeling and collaboration with Virginia Satir. The result of their collaboration was *Changing with Families,* in which a model for family therapy, based upon Bandler's and Grinder's modeling of Satir's success with families in therapy, is presented. Indeed, Virginia Satir's contributions to the development of NLP in family therapy cannot be overstated. After their collaboration with Satir, Bandler and Grinder began to model both their own successes with clients and their own abilities in creating useful behavioral models. From this map, they began to develop a series of patterns and techniques that became formalized as the discipline of Neuro-Linguistic Programming, and resulted in the publication of *Neuro-Linguistic Programming, Volume I,* co-authored with Robert Dilts.

Assisting in this process were several individuals who, beginning as students of Bandler and Grinder, have enhanced the development of NLP by their own modeling, research, teaching, and writing. They include Leslie Cameron-Bandler, author of *They Lived Happily Ever After,* David Gordon, author of *Therapeutic Metaphors,* Maribeth Anderson, co-author with David Gordon of *Phoenix: The Therapeutic Patterns of Milton H. Erickson, M.D.,* and the senior author of this work, Robert Dilts, co-author of *Neuro-Linguistic Programming, Volume I* and other works on NLP. The Society of Neuro-Linguistic Programming is the organization responsible for credentialing individuals in NLP™. The Society tests and certifies individuals as practitioners, master practitioners, and trainers of Neuro-Linguistic Programming, in order to insure that those who represent NLP will be highly trained and maintain rigorous standards of skill and professionalism.

PRESUPPOSITIONS OF NLP™

Like most disciplines, NLP has inherent in its structure a set of presuppositions that serve as a foundation for the development and implementation of the patterns and techniques that comprise NLP. We have found these presuppositions to be useful in securing professional and personal outcomes for our clients, as well as for ourselves.

1. *The map is not the territory.* The representations we use to organize our experience of the world are

not the world. They are neurological transformations that may or may not be accurate. As human beings, we input, output, and process information about the territory around us. That information is coded in terms of the five sensory systems: visual; auditory; kinesthetic (feelings); olfactory; and gustatory. The five senses are, in essence, the language of the human bio-computer, the brain. We refer to these five sensory systems as *"representational systems."* When people communicate, they tend to represent their experience of the world in words that have an origin in a particular sensory system (Grinder and Bandler, 1976; Cameron-Bandler, 1978; Dilts, et al., 1980). Each family member, for instance, may represent his experience of being appreciated with representations that have an origin in a sensory system different from another family member's system. These representations will be echoed in the linguistic patterns of the individuals. For example, one might hear statements such as: "I know I'm appreciated when I *see* someone smiling at me," "I know I'm appreciated when someone *tells* me," "I know I'm appreciated when someone *touches* me." The visual predicate *"see,"* the auditory predicate *"tells,"* and the kinesthetic predicate *"touches,"* all reflect an internal neurological pattern, or representational system, processed by the brain, that results in the sensory-based statement about being appreciated.

Being able to hear the sensory-based words, particularly predicates, that clients use, is an important tool in NLP. A list of words with contrasting non-referring or non-sensory specified predicates follows:

V	A	K	O,G	NON RE-FER-RING
see	hear	feel	smell	know
look	listen	grasp	taste	think
perspective	sounds	touch	sour	remember
focus	tone	grab	sweet	change
color (any)	tune	hold	salty	want
bright	tells	soft	stinks	need
picture	loud	warm	bitter	experience
shows	noise	handle	pungent	decide
imagine	amplify	rough	fragrant	negotiate
notice	say	smooth	aroma	pretend

Language, then, is a representation of our sensory representations: a map of another map. In NLP, we refer to language as *secondary experience* because it is even farther removed from the territory. Our *primary experience* are our actual ongoing, and stored, sensory perceptions of the world around us, brought in through our sense organs. We, then, use language as a trigger for isolated portions of primary experience.

It is extremely important for a family therapist (or anyone involved in human communication or behavior for that matter) to keep in mind that words have no inherent meaning in and of themselves. A word only has meaning in the individualized primary sensory representations it triggers in the speaker or listener.

Although language is critical to human communication, a great deal of distortion and slippage occurs in the coding of primary experience to secondary experience. Both the limiting and enriching effects of language have been discussed, at length, in *The Structure of Magic I and II; Patterns I and II; They*

Lived Happily Ever After; Changing with Families; and they will be discussed more in this chapter.

Let it suffice to say that, in NLP, we consider the highest quality information a professional communicator can get to be behavioral, as opposed to verbal. We might alter the old adage, "actions speak louder than words," to, "actions speak with much less slippage than words." In therapy, then, we consider it to be much more highly valued to get behavioral demonstrations than verbal descriptions to insure accurate communication.

2. *Mind and body are part of the same system and affect each other.* Human beings reflect their internal sensory processing not only by the sensory-based words that they use, but also by certain behavioral cues. *Eye movement patterns* are one of the most readily detectible behavioral cues. As illustrated by Grinder, DeLozier and Bandler (1977), Cameron-Bandler (1978), Bandler and Grinder (1979), and Dilts, et al. (1980), the following eye-movement patterns in most right-handed individuals (the eye movements of left-handed people are often reversed from left to right) are indicative of the following internal processing:

eyes, up and to the left	remembered imagery	(V^r)
eyes, up and to the right	constructed imagery	(V^c)
eyes, defocused in position	unspecified (either remembered or constructed) imagery	(V^i)
eyes, down and to the left	internal dialogue	(A_d)
eyes, level to the left	remembered sounds	(A^r)
eyes, level to the right	constructed sounds	(A^c)
eyes, down and to the right	kinesthetics	(K)

This can also be illustrated by the following figure:

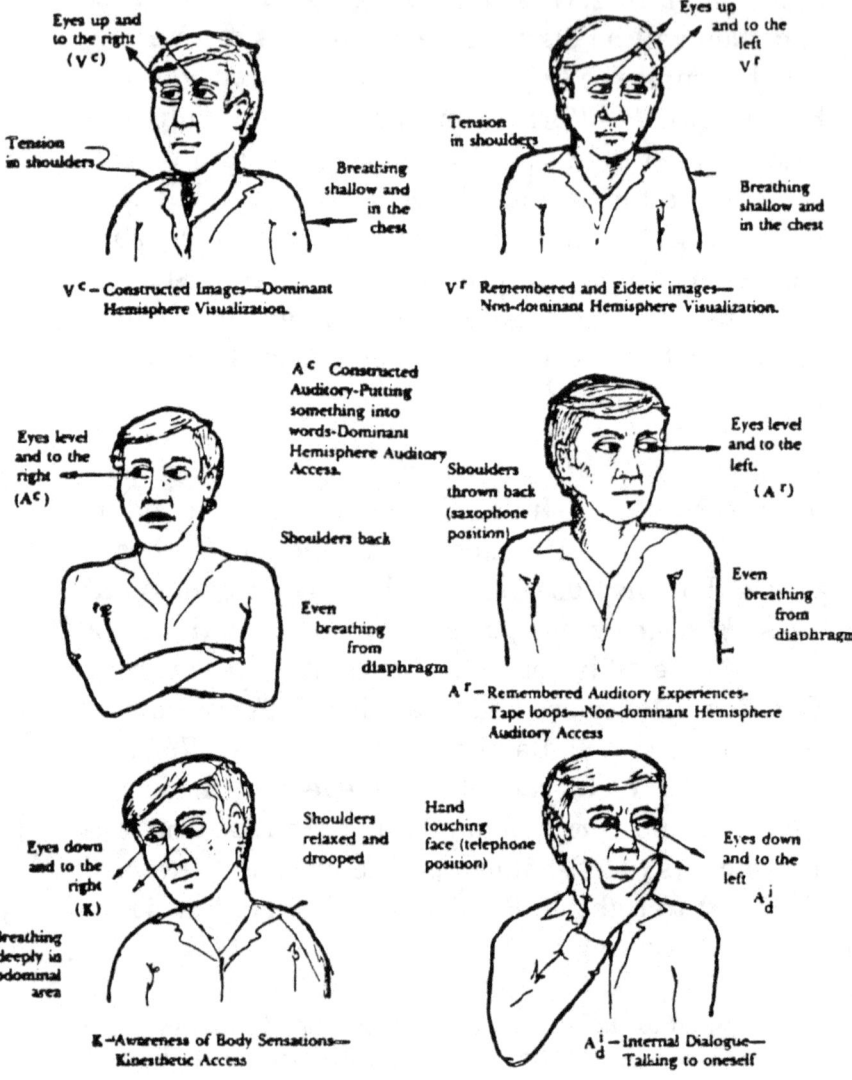

Figure 1. Accessing cues for typically wired right-handed person

Any behavioral cue that indicates processing of a certain sensory system is called an accessing cue. To illustrate, a husband might look up and to the left

(V^r) to *remember* the *look* on his wife's face when he gave her a gift. He might look up and to the right (V^c) to *construct an image* of the results of a surprise trip he is planning to take her on, and down and to the left (A_d) to *talk to himself* internally about either picture. In order to *remember* his wife *telling* him, "I love you," he may look straight and level to the left (A^r). *Constructing* various ways to *tell* his wife how much he appreciates her, he might look straight and level to the right (A^c). He may look down and to the right (K) to access the *feeling* of being loved.

Other behavioral accessing cues and indicators are speech tempo (fast-V, slow-K, in between-A), speech tone (high-V, low-K, in between-A), breathing rate (shallow-V, deep-K, in between-A), breathing position (high in the chest-V, low in the stomach-K, in-between or diaphragm breathing-A), and head tilt or "phone postures" (indicating auditory access).

Just as the functioning of the mind is reflected in behavioral accessing cues in the body, so accessing a particular behavioral cue can affect the functioning of the mind. To illustrate, it is possible to affect the state of consciousness of an individual, who constantly *looks down* and to the right (K) and is caught in bad feelings, by simply directing that individual to *look up and to the left* (V^r), and visualize positive experiences.

3. *Individual skills are a function of the development and sequencing of representational systems.* We firmly believe that any skill, talent, or ability that an individual has can be broken down into its representational system components, and taught to anyone who does not have severe physiological or neurological damage. We have discovered that chil-

dren labeled as learning disabled often have limited development of some representational system. Some of these children, for instance, will have underdeveloped visual-remembered and visual-constructed systems. Dyslexia, for example, is the inability to visualize words. Since schools teach subjects that require a well-developed ability to visualize, these children have a difficult time learning. As an illustration, good spellers, typically, have a stored visual-remembered image for each word they have learned to spell; poorer spellers, on the other hand, tend to sound words out. Auditory spellers often experience difficulty, since the English language is not always spelled phonetically. In trying to spell "phonetics," phonetically, for instance, one may easily come up with a spelling like "funetix." We work with poor spellers to help them develop a better visual-remembered imagery capacity. In as few as one or two sessions, we can teach poor spellers to have the visual-remembered imagery ability of a good speller. In the same way, we can teach someone, who has little or no access to their feelings, to develop their visceral kinesthetic representational system.

Everything that individuals do, from learning to decision making, from motivation to creativity, from athletic ability to the ability to distinguish what is real from what is not, is a result of the development and sequencing of representational system activity, what we call "strategies" (Cameron-Bandler, 1978; Dilts, et al., 1980). As an illustration, a woman comes to you and says the following:

(Eyes down left) I *told* myself I need to do something about my marriage, and, then, (eyes up right) I *pictured* myself getting a divorce, but (eyes down right, then down left) something *told* me that didn't *feel* right. So, I (eyes remain down left) *told* myself, "you have to do something." So, I (eyes up right) *pictured* coming to a therapist and (eyes down right, then down left) something *told* me that that *felt* like the right thing to do. So, here I am.

This is a brief example of a decision strategy. We have developed a calculus for notating strategies, the sequence of representational systems. Using the notation system, the above client's decision strategy would be notated as follows:

$$\underline{A_d \rightarrow V^c \rightarrow K/K} \rightarrow A_d \rightarrow \text{Exit}$$

She tells herself she needs to make a decision (A_d), pictures an option (V^c), and then compares the feeling she has about the picture (K) with an internally stored feeling of rightness (/K). If the option has the same feeling as the feeling of rightness she tells herself (A_d) it feels right and exits. If the option does not have the same feeling as the feeling of rightness, she tells herself so, and cycles back through the strategy until she finds an option that does have the same feeling as the feeling of rightness. Her ability to make a decision is directly dependent on her ability to visually construct options within the sequence of representational systems in her decision strategy.

We can utilize this decision strategy if we want to facilitate her decision making process. If she is in the midst of making a decision and is having a difficult time creating options, we can provide her with options by verbally *painting clear pictures* of those options, using visually-oriented, sensory-grounded words. The goal is to insure that she has a very clear visually-constructed image of the options we present to her. (For more on NLP strategy technology, see *NLP I.*)

4. *The meaning of any communication is the response it elicits, regardless of the intent of the communicator* (Bandler and Grinder, 1979). When we are in the context of communicating with another human being, each one of our behaviors, both verbal and non-verbal, elicits a response in that other human being, which often is one we did not actually intend to elicit.

How many times have you heard a statement like, "I was only trying to help," or "I was just trying to give some advice," or "I keep telling her that I love her, but she just gets upset," from a family member after he, or she, has just done, or said, something that caused another family member to burst into tears or get angry? The father who gets irritated and yells at his child, while that child is struggling with homework, may do so in an attempt to help the child learn. He may not realize that his behavior is getting the opposite of the response he intends to get. When a husband says to his wife, "Don't be so angry with me," and she responds by yelling, "I'm not angry!", she has missed an important point. Regardless of whether or not she was angry, that *was* the meaning to her husband of what she was doing and saying. Both of them could learn a great deal from this interaction. The wife could learn that if she wants to communicate something different, she needs to change her delivery, to more accurately convey her internal state. The husband could learn to reinterpret the communication signals from his wife.

Sometimes people will communicate two messages simultaneously. Often you will hear statements like, "Damn it, I told you I loved you!" Here the communicator may be experiencing both love and anger, but other family members may only respond to the signals that communicate anger. Being able to detect, separate, and sort out multiple communications into their pure form is an important part of the therapist's role, and will be discussed in more detail later.

Thus, it is of utmost importance that the client and therapist come to the realization that the significance of a communication is what is being received on the other end. Most people communicate to others in a way that is perfectly understandable to themselves, but may miss the point of communicating, altogether. An effective communicator is not an individual with a good command of language and delivery, but rather an individual who has the sensory experience and flexibility to make the response they elicit match the intended meaning of his communication.

5. *Human beings are capable of one-trial learning.* This is the presupposition, underlying the principle of "anchoring" (Cameron-Bandler, 1978; Bandler and Grinder, 1979; Dilts, et al., 1980). Anchoring is the term we use when referring to the learned association between an external stimulus and an internal response, or between one response and another. If I am working with a couple, and elicit an internal re-

sponse in the husband of confidence that he can get what he wants in the relationship, and simultaneously touch him on the shoulder, then each time I trigger the stimulus of the touch on the shoulder, he will tend to re-experience the response of confidence.

Anchoring is the operationalizing of classical conditioning in the therapeutic context. According to Cameron-Bandler (1978):

> Many therapists already utilize this process by using a special voice tone and tempo, when doing a guided fantasy or hypnosis. This voice tone becomes an anchor for the altered states that are experienced when it is used. In Gestalt chair work, too, each of the two chairs becomes an anchor for a different emotional state and the client changes radically, as he moves from one chair to the other. (p. 105)

Often family members become anchored to each other in "calibrated loops." As an illustration, a husband, as he is talking to his wife, increases the volume in his voice. As his volume increases, she becomes angry. As she becomes angry she physically turns away from him. He feels ignored, so, in order to get her attention, he talks louder, and so on. His external behavior (EB) of loudness elicits an internal response (IR), in her, of anger. Her anger changes her external behavior (EB) and she turns away from him, an act that elicits an internal response (IR) in him of feeling ignored. His feeling ignored changes his external behavior (EB) and he raises the volume of his voice, and so on. Such a loop can often result in a snowball effect when both behaviors and internal responses escalate far past the point of usefulness. This interaction can be mapped as follows:

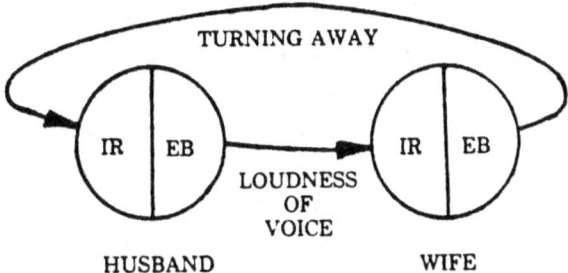

Thus his rise in volume becomes an anchor for the internal response of anger in her. Her turning away from him becomes an anchor for his internal response of feeling ignored. This, then, is a *calibrated loop*. Part of the therapist's task is to break useless calibrated loops in families that result in a series of negative internal responses, elicited in family members. More will be said about this in the techniques section.

6. *Individuals have all the resources they need to achieve their desired outcomes.* When we talk about resources, we are referring to the internal responses and external behaviors that family members need to get desired responses from one another. The resources that family members need are usually available to them in other contexts. It's the therapist's task to access these resources from other contexts, and make them available to individuals, in the family therapy context.

Some internal responses that serve as resources in family therapy are the experiences love, trust, support, confidence, respect, acceptance, and appreciation. One way individuals lose access to resources is when these resources become hidden or distorted through language. Because the words we use to describe or communicate our experience are not the experiences themselves, a tremendous amount of slippage and ambiguity can occur, as family members communicate. Family members will often state that they want more "love," more "support," more "respect," and so on. The linguistic label we place on words like "love," "support," "respect," is nominalization (Bandler and Grinder, 1975; Cameron-Bandler, 1978; Green, 1979). Nominalization is the linguistic mechanism by which complex experiences that occur over time are represented as some *thing* that occurs in a single moment in time, or as a thing rather than a process. To say that you've lost your husband's "respect" is like saying that you've lost his "watch." You are referring to an ongoing process, action, or relationship as if it were an object or thing. Such distortion can produce profound interference in good communication. One of the therapist's tasks, in accessing resources, is to denominalize these words into the experiences or processes that they represent. For example, a client who wants more "support" from his wife would be asked to specify what specific behaviors and actions of his wife demonstrate to him that she is being supportive. He may be asked, "What, specifically, would your wife be doing right now, if she were supporting you?" Here, the therapist has put the noun "support" back into verb form to recover the specific actions associated with the word and thus reduce the distortion. For other methods for both recognizing and denominalizing nominalizations, and for dealing with other problematic linguistic phenomena, the reader is referred to *The Structure of Magic, Volume I.*

The denominalization process presents one method of accessing resources. The practitioner of NLP has several other methods at his disposal to access both internal responses, such as love or trust, that family members want, and those behaviors that family members can utilize to successfully elicit desired emotional responses or behaviors from other family members. For instance, clients can be asked the following: to remember a time when they experienced a certain response or utilized a certain behavior; to demonstrate the response or behavior in the ongoing context; to think of a time in the future when they know they will or think they might experience the response or to think of a behavior they could utilize in the future; or to think of someone they know who has the response or utilizes a successful behavior. Because mind and body are part of the same system (as stated previously), as people access these reference experiences, they will begin to manifest and recapitulate portions of those experiences in the present. These manifestations can then be anchored and utilized.

7. *Behavior is geared toward adaptation.* This has two corollaries. a) Individuals make the best choices available to them at any point in time—if given a better choice they will take it. b) Underlying every behavior is a *positive intent*. Anyone who has ever worked with a family will realize the tremendous amount of *secondary gain* that often accompanies problematic behaviors. Behaviors such as hyperactivity, alcoholism, anorexia, learning disabilities, sexual dysfunction, and obesity, may serve the positive functions of getting attention, protection, approval, or escape from other family members. Many

family therapists and researchers, notably Bateson (1973), Laing (1964), Haley (1973), Erickson (1967), and Satir (1972), have shown that behaviors of individual family members that appear bizarre, and even crazy, become completely understandable when viewed in terms of that individual's relationship with the family system. One of the goals of NLP in family therapy is to discover the positive intents of family members' behaviors, and find alternatives to those behaviors that secure the same positive intent as existing patterns of behavior, without any of the negative by-products.

In the previous example of a calibrated loop, the husband who increases the volume of his voice made the best choice available to him in that context. If it's important to him to be respected—and the way he knows that people respect him is that they *look* at him when he talks—then his underlying intent, to be respected, is positive. If he knew that his wife would look at him if he lowered his volume and touched her simultaneously, our premise is that this would be the best choice available to him, and he would utilize it.

8. *There is no substitute in communications for clean, active, open, sensory channels to know what response you are eliciting at any moment in time.* Many family members literally do not perceive the impact that their behavior is having on other family members. The first step in creating positive change in a family is to have the family members become aware of just what responses, both positive and negative, their behavior is eliciting in other family members. Often, individuals in a family system respond to their memories or projections of a family member,

rather than to the ongoing evidence that the individual's behavior or actions are different. Similarly, individuals limit and curb their behavior around others, because of beliefs drawn from experiences that happened long ago, but have never been retested or reevaluated. Illustrations of this are: the child who never grows up in his parents' eyes, or the son who is afraid to make decisions on his own because his father got angry at him when he, the son, made wrong decisions in the past. Teaching family members to see and hear the responses they are eliciting, as they communicate, can often create lasting changes in a short period of time.

In NLP training seminars, we teach participants how to detect visually subtle changes in another's eye movements, postural and gestural complexes, skin color, lower lip size, muscle tones, and breathing rate and position, and how to detect auditorally subtle changes in another's voice tone, tempo, timbre, pitch, and volume. We call these changes *minimal cues,* as they tend to be typically unconscious but powerful triggers for recurrent patterns of behavior. Our students are then taught how to associate and store the sets of minimal cues that are paired with concurrent responses in their clients. Changes in these patterns of behavior often lead to some of the most profound and lasting changes within the family system.

9. *The element in a system that has the most flexibility will be the controlling, or catalytic, element in that system.* This is the *Law of Requisite Variety* (Ashby, 1956). Stated more simply, *if what you're doing is not eliciting the responses you want, then do something different.* Since behaviors elicit responses,

if you change your behavior, you will get a different response. It is truly remarkable to observe, over and over again in the context of family therapy, that even though family members will have proved to themselves that what they are doing consistently does not get them the responses they want, they continue doing that same thing. In NLP, we do not think that the old adage, "If you don't succeed, try, try again," is always the best advice. Our advice is rather, "If you don't succeed, then keep trying something *different,* until you do succeed."

One of the authors worked with a woman who complained that her husband never listened to her. For years, she said, her husband would be late to pick her up or pick up one of their children, even though she would "look him straight in the eye" and tell him "loud and clear" when to be there. The author pointed out to her that for years she'd been doing this same behavior, and for years he had consistently been late. It was now time to try something different. The author suggested that instead of looking him in the eye, the next time she wanted him to be somewhere on time, she sneak up behind him, and instead of telling him loud and clear, she whisper in his ear. Certainly, she had nothing to lose. The woman tried the new approach with much success and generalized the principle of flexibility to other areas where they had been experiencing miscommunication.

Flexibility is at the root of such important processes as creativity, adaptability, and choice. In family therapy, our premise is that the more flexible family members are, the more they will be able to

Applications of Neuro-Linguistic Programming

elicit the responses they want from other family members.

THERAPIST'S ROLE

The Neuro-Linguistic Programmer's role in family therapy is to implement a three-step process (Cameron-Bandler, 1978):

1. Gathering information concerning the clients' present state and desired state, and establishing rapport with the clients.

2. Evolving the clients from their present state to their desired state.

3. Future pacing—integrating the desired state of experience into their ongoing behavior. (p. 26)

Establishing *rapport* is an essential step in the family therapy process.

> To effectively gather information, or begin a process of change, it will always be important to establish rapport between yourself and your client, at both the conscious and unconscious level. An invaluable technique for doing just this is to generate verbal and nonverbal behavior that matches that of your client. This is called "matching." The client's subjective experience becomes one of being really understood. After all, you are speaking their language, verbally and nonverbally. (Cameron-Bandler, 1978, p. 64.)

It has been stated previously that it is important for the Neuro-Linguistic Programmer to be able to hear the sensory-based words that a client uses. One method of establishing verbal rapport with a client is to match the sensory-based words a client uses (Grinder and Bandler, 1976; Bandler and Grinder,

1979; Cameron-Bandler, 1978). If a client says to you, "Things aren't *looking* very good for my husband and me. I just can't *see* any future in our staying together," she is using visual predicates. In order to establish rapport with her, you would use visually-based words in your communications to her. You might then say, "I'm beginning to get the *picture,* but perhaps you could bring into *focus* what it is you want in coming to *see* me."

We have often found that in family systems individuals are highly specialized in using one representational system (Grinder and Bandler, 1976; Cameron-Bandler, 1978). Thus, in a family system, some members may use primarily visual words, while others may use primarily kinesthetic or auditory words to represent their experience. They are, in essence, speaking different languages. It is the task of the therapist to translate experiences from one representational system to another, so family members can better understand each other. One of the authors worked with a family in which the husband was highly visual and the wife highly kinesthetic. She complained that he never *touched* her when they were in public, and as a consequence, she *felt* like he wasn't proud to be with her. He couldn't understand her response, because people could, obviously, *see* that they were together. In order to help him understand his wife's response, the therapist translated her kinesthetic experience into a visual one through the following statement." "You realize that when you don't touch Nancy in public, it's like having someone you care about not wanting to be *seen* in your company."

Other ways of establishing rapport with a client verbally are to match the client's voice in tone and tempo. To establish rapport nonverbally, the therapist can match the head tilt, body posture, breathing rate, and gestures of a client. The importance of establishing rapport with members of a family cannot be overstated. Each member of the family must have some rapport with the therapist, or the process of helping the family can be greatly inhibited. Milton Erickson was a master at reaching each client in his model of the world, to establish rapport. He did this consistently by matching behavior of clients. Erickson (Haley, 1973) relates a story of working with a family in which the identified patient was a ten-year-old son who was a bed wetter. The boy was brought into Erickson's office by the parents.

> They laid him face down in my office. I shoved the parents out the door. The boy was yelling.
> When the boy paused to catch his breath, I said, "That's a godam hell of a way to do, I don't like it a damn bit." It surprised him that I would say this. He hesitated while taking that breath, and I told him he might as well go ahead and yell again. He let out a yell, and when he paused to take a breath, I let out a yell. He turned to look at me, and I said, "It's my turn." Then I said, "Now it's your turn," so he yelled again. I yelled again, and then said it was his turn again. Then I said, "Now, we can go right on taking turns, but that will get awfully tiresome. I'd rather take my turn by sitting down in that chair. There's a vacant one over there." So I took my turn sitting down in my chair, and he took his turn by sitting down in the other chair. (p. 200)

Thus Erickson established rapport with a hostile young client, and persuaded him to sit down in a chair by artfully matching and utilizing a particular behavior, that of yelling.

Simultaneously with establishing rapport, the therapist gathers information concerning the present state and desired state of the family. The *present state* can be defined as that set of factors that brought the family in for therapy. The *desired state* can be defined as those responses or behaviors that family members would like to be able to elicit from one another. (More will be said about the present state and desired state in following sections of this chapter.)

The major tools that the therapist uses to gather information about the present state and desired state are clean, active, open sensory channels. We believe that the highest quality information is behavioral. When working with a family, it is extremely important to keep in mind that the *map is not the territory*. The perceptions of family members about their system are not the system itself. Many subtle, but impactful, minimal cues, anchors, linguistic, and behavioral patterns exist in the family system that are far below the awareness of individual family members. Rather than rely on descriptions from persons inside the family system, the Neuro-Linguistic Programmer will concentrate much more on eliciting and carefully observing patterns of family interaction. Thus, the therapist looks and listens for demonstrations of the present state behaviors of family members that result in negative kinesthetic responses, or unwanted behaviors from other family members. It is our task to discover what calibrated loops exist, what anchors exist, and what incongruencies exist in the family system that make it possible for family members to fail to get what they want. In the example cited earlier of the husband whose increase in volume and tonality elicited a negative response from his wife, the therapist needed the sensory experience to hear the rise in volume and tonality in the husband's voice, and to see the negative response elicited in the wife.

It is also our task to look and listen for demonstrations of the desired state. If one family member wants to be able to elicit desired responses or behaviors from a second family member, we want to be able to detect, with our sensory apparatus, when that response or behavior is elicited. For the task of gathering high quality information the Neuro-Linguistic Programmer completely disregards the adage, "It is more easily said than done." Rather, the programmer operates off the inverse wisdom. For the purpose of getting high quality information we fully believe it is "more easily done than said." An excellent information gathering technique (and powerful covert therapeutic tactic) is to ask each family member to direct himself, or herself, and the other family members in a "role play" of how everyone would act "if" the desired outcomes with the family had been accomplished. Such a scenario gives the programmer a number of important opportunities:

1. It allows the programmer to *see* and *hear* a high quality example of the desired state, rather than have to sort out and make sense out of slippery verbal descriptions.

2. In acting out the desired state, even though they are only acting "as if" it were so, the family is actually, behaviorally, installing new patterns of behavior. The family has the opportunity to behaviorally evaluate what the desired state will be like. Often family members will unconsciously install the new behaviors immediately, because the positive effects are so obvious. Likewise, any behaviors or responses that

are inappropriate or unecological to the family system will be immediately evident.

3. It gives the programmer an easy opportunity to anchor pieces of behavior or internal responses that may be invaluable later, and to fine-tune, add to, or alter patterns of behavior *as* they occur.

When employing such a technique, of course, it is imperative that the programmer fully use his sensory capabilities to make sure that the appropriate tonal and tempo qualities, facial, gestural, and postural expressions are being demonstrated in the "role play."

When working with any client, but most critically when a family system is involved, a therapist must pay a tremendous amount of attention to the ecological impact of any change or desired outcome on the interpersonal systems of which the client is a part (for example, work, family, friends, etc.). If a wife comes in and asks for the ability to be more assertive with her husband, the impact of that outcome should be carefully examined. If she is given exactly what she wants, assertive behavior, without sensitivity to her husband's internal state or the sensory experience to detect and respond to what that assertive behavior is eliciting in her husband, she may unnecessarily alienate him or end up with a broken jaw. Therefore, before any attempt is made at actually giving individual family members what they request, the therapist should gather high quality information about the repercussions of the desired state. Often the ongoing problematic behavior(s) will serve an important function in the existing ecology of the family system, or will have an important positive by-product that must be preserved by any new options interjected into the system.

We believe that the following questions indicate the minimum amount of information necessary for the therapist to gather, before actually working to change the existing family system. Note that although these are stated as questions, the therapist will want to gather information and examples by observing family behavior in context to get the highest quality answers. What people say they do and what they do are not always the same thing.

Present State

1. What are you experiencing now? (present state)

2. In what contexts do you experience it?

3. Is there ever a time when you don't experience it? (counter-example)

4. What positive benefits does it get for you? (secondary gain)

Desired State

1. What, specifically, do you want? (outcome)

2. How would you know if you had it? What would constitute a demonstration of the desired state? (complex equivalence)

3. What would happen if you got it? (ecology)

4. What stops you from getting it?

5. In what contexts do you want it?

6. Are there any contexts in which you don't want it? (counter-example)

7. Has there ever been a time when you had it? How did you know that you had it? What constituted

a demonstration of the desired state? (complex equivalence)

8. Do you remember a time when you had it? What was it like when you had it? What will it be like to have it? What is it like to have it? (test information)

A few of the above questions require explanation. The purpose of the test-information questions is to get the client to access the desired state. They will also elicit the set of minimal cues associated with the desired state. This gives the therapist test criteria for the presence of the desired state. The ecology questions are designed to elicit any negative by-products of achieving the desired state, and to insure that any positive by-products associated with the present state will be preserved in the desired state.

When clients respond verbally to one of the above questions, they are responding incompletely. Since words are only representations of experience, and can never be a complete expression, there will always be missing pieces about the clients' experience in any verbalization they might offer. In additon to using sensory awareness to recover the missing pieces, there is a powerful verbal tool, in NLP, to help obtain more complete representations of the clients' experience. The meta model (Bandler and Grinder, 1975), gives an explicit set of questions to ask, to elicit more information about the clients' experience. So when the therapist asks the client, "What do you want?" and he responds, "I want to be loved," the therapist using the meta model is able to identify that a linguistic violation, or deletion, has occurred and then asks, "By whom, specifically?" Thus essential information about what the client wants is recovered. A full presentation of the meta model patterns, violations, and challenges is beyond the scope of this chapter. Instead we refer the reader to *The Structure of Magic, Volume I* and *They Lived Happily Ever After.*

After rapport is established, and information about the present state and desired state is elicited, the therapist moves the system from the present state to the desired state with the techniques of change developed in NLP. After the desired state is achieved, it is future-paced or integrated into the on-going behavior of the clients, in the contexts in which it is needed. More will be said about techniques and future-pacing in future sections.

CLIENT'S ROLE

All that is required of a client by a Neuro-Linguistic Programmer is that he, she, or they have an outcome they would like to achieve, or have something that they would like to be different in their lives. Note that this does not mean that the client has to have a problem or that there has to be something wrong, only that the client has a desired state. The purpose of NLP in therapy is not to "fix" "broken" people (there are too many presuppositions, distortions, and arbitrary standards in such an approach), but rather to evolve people to where they would like to be. For example, NLP is not just for the learning disabled, but is equally applicable to those who learn well and want to learn better.

Since one of the primary presuppositions, on which NLP is based, is that people respond with the best choices available to them at any point in time, it is evident that the major role of the client, in the therapeutic applications of NLP, is to respond. However, in NLP it is not considered the client's responsibility to respond in any prescribed way. It is the programmer's task to establish rapport with the client, to go to the client's model of the world, rather than have the client come to the therapist's.

One of the goals of the programmer is to have clients chunk their experience and desired outcomes in terms of their representational systems and sensory experience. If the client is unable to, or has difficulty in doing this, however, it is not considered to be the client's fault. In NLP, there is no such thing as a resistant, stupid, or incapable person. Since, in NLP, we believe that the meaning of your communication is the response you elicit, irrespective of your intent, if a programmer asks a client for a particular response, and the client does not respond appropriately, it is an indication that the programmer has not paced the client's model of the world fully enough to elicit the desired response. To say that a client is resistant is only a statement about the inflexibility of the therapist.

Note that when we say "response," we do not mean only consciously willful responses. Many of the patterns most important to the NLP programmer are those that are below the client's level of conscious awareness, and are the result of activities that take place below awareness. The programmer is most interested in those patterns that the client is compelled to do and, more often than not, is unaware that he *is* compelled to do. Also, since in NLP we are more interested in the formal properties of the patterns rather than the content of the patterns, in many cases a conscious report of the content is not even necessary. There is a therapeutic process in

NLP called "Secret Therapy" (see *Frogs Into Princes, They Lived Happily Ever After,* and *NLP I*), in which the programmer never knows the content of the client's problem or outcome. An arbitrary name, like "red" or "purple," is assigned to the presenting problem or outcome. Since it is the sensory-specific minimal cues and patterns that the programmer elicits and utilizes in relationship to the presenting behavior, the content of the pattern need never be made overtly explicit to the programmer (and sometimes not even the client).

In the most general sense, the Neuro-Linguistic Programmer views every client as a system of uniquely interconnected representations and motor patterns (that is, internal responses and external behaviors). Each system has infinite potential, the expression of which is determined by the combinations and sequences of representations with motor patterns. What makes the system operate in a successful and adaptive fashion is a function of three properties:

1. An explicit representation of the outcome being worked toward.

2. Clean, active sensory channels, so that the system's progress toward the outcome may be perceived, assessed, and responded to.

3. Flexibility of both internal responses and external behavior, so that the outcome may be worked toward and achieved in many diverse contexts and situations.

Difficulties occur when any one of these properties is deficient with respect to the current outcomes of the client. It is the programmer's responsibility to identify in which sector the client is impoverished, and assist the client in adding choices.

Present State: Problems of Clients

Traditional psychotheologies have often grouped together individuals with similar problematic behaviors under certain diagnostic labels. These labels are as general as the behaviors to which they refer, as in "psychosis," or as specific as "anorexia nervosa." As we have stated previously, however, the "map is not the territory." The word "schizophrenic" does not contain the complex uniqueness of the human being that this label represents. Often, however, the unique territory—that of the human being—is treated as if he was the label. This has resulted in several suppositions, in some corners of the world of psychotherapy, such as "schizophrenics are incurable," or behavior is "crazy or sick," or "they'll never be able to live a normal life." Unfortunately, these suppositions only serve to elicit negative responses in therapists about the people they treat. Such negative responses often prevent the therapist from establishing rapport, or understanding the client's model of the world, and limits the therapist's flexibility.

In Neuro-Linguistic Programming, we believe that each human being is unique, and has a unique set of external behaviors and internal responses. Rather than use diagnostic labels, we find it much more useful to define client problem areas in terms of behaviors and responses. We want to know what behaviors of family members trigger what negative internal responses in other family members. We want to know what desired behaviors and responses family members have difficulty eliciting from one another.

As stated previously, we believe that every behavior and response is the best choice an individual has available to him. We have found that chunking problems in terms of behaviors and responses, and believing that these behaviors and responses are the best available choices to our clients, increases our ability to establish rapport, to be flexible in our behavior, and thus, to more effectively help our clients secure their desired outcomes.

Desired State—Goals of the Therapeutic Process

As we mentioned in a previous section, the primary goal of NLP, in the therapeutic context, is to assist clients in enriching their representational maps and behavioral outputs to achieve a) an explicit representation of their outcomes; b) the open and active sensory awareness of where their behavior is leading them, with respect to their outcomes; and c) enough flexibility of internal responses and external behaviors so that they can adapt their behavior to the changing contexts in which they may find themselves.

Neuro-Linguistic Programming is, obviously, highly outcome-oriented. Although sensory awareness and behavioral flexibility are absolutely critical resources for anyone to live an adaptive and well-functioning life, they are only tools by which outcomes can be achieved. Thus, the initial, and most important step, in any therapeutic interaction (or any human endeavor for that matter) is the identification and definition of the outcome. In NLP, we believe that 70–90% of the impact of any therapeutic process is in the establishment of the outcome.

Perhaps the best way to communicate to the reader the goals of NLP in the therapeutic process is to list the well-formedness conditions that we impose on our clients' definitions of their outcomes. In NLP, we have met our initial therapeutic goal when a client has identified and is working toward an outcome that satisfies the following well-formedness conditions.

1. *The outcome must be stated in positive terms.* In NLP, we believe that it is practically and logically impossible to give someone the negation of an experience. Thus if a client says, "I want to not feel so anxious anymore," or, "I don't want to be so critical of myself," or, "I want to be less upset at my children," the programmer's first task is to find out what the client, in fact, does want in place of the negative experience. The programmer might ask, for example, "If you weren't anxious, what would you be feeling instead?" or, "What would you like to be doing to yourself in place of being critical?" or, "What would things be like if you were able to be less upset with your children?" It is in general much easier to design a way for a client to operate toward a positive outcome than away from a negative one.

2. *The outcome must be testable and demonstrable in sensory experience.* The only way in which setting an outcome is going to be useful to anyone is if you are explicitly able to perceive and evaluate progress towards it, as you attempt to achieve it. Identifying and defining a demonstration of the desired state is as beneficial to the programmer as it is to the client. It will give the therapist an explicit reference to

Applications of Neuro-Linguistic Programming

evaluate his own progress, as well as the client's. The programmer will minimally want to establish two sets of criteria, or tests, for the client's outcome: a) one set for the ongoing therapeutic context; and b) one set for the client to use outside the office. For example, the therapist may ask, "What will be a demonstration to you and me, here, today, that you can achieve the outcome(s) that you want for yourself?" and "What will be a demonstration to you that you have achieved (or are achieving) your outcome(s) with your spouse (children, family, boss, or others)?" The programmer then has an explicit way of knowing when he has been successful with the client.

3. *The desired state must be initiated and maintained by the client.* One of the major goals of NLP is to put the locus of control, with respect to achieving the outcome, with the client. Thus, if a woman comes in and states, "I want my husband to stop ignoring me," her statement does not satisfy any of the criteria listed so far for a well-formed outcome. In this case the programmer would want to first ask "What would your husband be doing if he weren't ignoring you?" (getting a positive statement of the outcome). Here, the therapist would want to get a sensory-based description of how the husband would be paying attention to the wife in her model of the world. Some satisfactory answers might be, "He would *talk* to me more about the children," "He would *hold* me and *touch* me more often," "He would *notice* and *comment* on how I *look* more often." The programmer would then want to put the control of the outcome in the client's hands by asking, "What could you do (have you done, are you doing) to get your husband to

want to talk to you, (touch you, notice you) more often?" The programmer would then want to help the client install the appropriate flexibility of behavior to achieve the outcome. To insure that the behavior is appropriate, the programmer would also ask, "What will be a demonstration to you and me that you have the resources you need to get your husband to pay attention to you in the way(s) that you've specified?"

4. *The outcome must be explicitly and appropriately contextualized.* Many times people state their outcomes in the form of absolutes, or what we call "universal quantifiers" (Bandler and Grinder, 1975; Cameron-Bandler, 1978). In such cases, it is implied that the outcome is wanted in all contexts and for all circumstances, when in actuality the unwanted behavior may be totally useful and appropriate in some situations, and conversely, the desired behavior may be totally inappropriate and problematic in other situations. Therefore, if someone says, "I want to stop yelling at my children," the programmer would want to ask, "Are there any times in which yelling at your children would be appropriate?" or, "Are there any times when you would *want* to yell at your children?" Likewise, if someone says, "I want to feel better about punishing my children," the programmer would want to ask, "Are there any situations or conditions in which you wouldn't want to feel good about punishing your children?" Here the programmer is specifying the appropriate boundaries and limits for desired and undesirable outcomes. The goal of NLP is not to take away responses or behaviors or to simply substitute one behavior for another, but to *give the client more choices.* To insure

Applications of Neuro-Linguistic Programming

that the choices available to the client are going to be the best ones, the programmer will often have to contextualize desired outcomes to specific times, persons, places, activities, and so on.

5. *The desired state must preserve any positive by-products of the present state.* The positive by-products of unwanted behaviors are best illustrated in what are referred to as habits (smoking, overeating, heavy drinking, etc.). Many smokers, for instance, smoke to calm themselves down when they are nervous. A surprising number of smokers smoke to remind themselves, and compel themselves, to breathe deeply. If a smoker quits, and no substitute or choice has been installed by which the smoker may relax and remember to breathe deeply, he will experience a great amount of difficulty and discomfort. When the positive by-product is not explicitly accounted for in the desired state, people will often find substitute behaviors that become just as problematic. For example, people may take to overeating or drinking, instead of smoking, when they are nervous, or some other form of symptom substitution. Many people who are overweight unconsciously feel that if they lost weight and became more attractive, they would not have the resources to say "no" if they were approached by a member of the opposite sex. If the desired state does not include adequate resources to insulate against such possibilities, the client may lose weight and his marriage at the same time.

6. *The desired state must be ecologically sound.* This well-formedness condition, involving the preservation of the positive by-product(s), obviously relates to the previous one. Certainly, the failure to

preserve a positive by-product would be unecological. The purpose of including this condition, however, is mainly to orient the therapist and the client toward considering possible future impacts of the outcome, in order to prevent the opening of a Pandora's box. Many outcomes, even though they preserve the positive by-product of the present state, lead to situations and behaviors that may be both unexpected and unwanted. A colleague of the authors, for instance, once helped "cure" a schizophrenic girl. Six months after the girl's re-integration into the family, however, the girl's father, who had "desperately wanted, and supported," his daughter's treatment, had, for all intents and purposes, become an alcoholic. In family systems especially, the repercussions of any desired outcome should be explored in detail so they may be prepared for and handled appropriately. The programmer will want to know what the client, as well as the client's family members, will stand to lose, as well as gain, upon the achievement of any outcome. Sometimes the shockwave through a system that results from a change in one member's behavior may create an outcome that is more problematic than the initial presenting problem.

TECHNIQUES

The function of any Neuro-Linguistic Programming technique is to enrich, or add to, one of the three properties of effective behavior we have listed previously: a) an explicit representation of the outcome; b) sensory experience; and c) flexibility of internal responses and external behavior.

The many, many explicit techniques and procedures that make up the behavioral technology of NLP are presented in the ever-growing number of books that represent the development of the field of Neuro-Linguistic Programming (see reference section). There are also many techniques that have not been transformed into written representations, and many still in the process of being refined and developed. A complete presentation is far beyond the scope and purpose of this chapter. What is presented here is a limited representation of the NLP family therapy model. Any attempt to present the model in its entirety would neither be useful nor practical. Rather, what we are presenting are the applications of some of the aspects of the overall NLP model to the context of family therapy. Some of the techniques that we have briefly discussed in the progress of this chapter are:

1. Identifying and matching the most commonly used sensory-based words and predicates of the client for the purposes of creating rapport, and insuring understanding between the therapist and the client(s).

2. Pacing, through the matching and mirroring of postural, gestural, and facial positions and movements, and of voice tone and tempo qualities of the client(s), to contribute to the rapport between client and therapist.

3. Translating experiences expressed through one representational modality to another, to help increase understanding between family members.

4. Observation and utilization of sensory accessing cues and minimal cues, to help understand and pace the client's typical processing strategies for organiz-

ing and making sense of his experiences, and communications received from others.

5. Helping to build new representational possibilities and capabilities in clients, through the use of sensory-specific language and systematic use of accessing cues.

6. Helping to increase the sensory awareness of clients so they can more accurately and immediately perceive and evaluate the effects of their behavior on other family members.

7. Identify and sort out multiple (incongruent) communications in clients to help reduce misunderstanding and confusion.

8. Establish anchors and triggers for positive experiences and resources that occur in one context, and re-trigger or re-sequence them in other situations where they are not yet available to the client. Thus, those behaviors and responses may serve as resources in other contexts as well.

9. Identify and break unuseful "calibrated loops" between family members to add more flexibility and choice in responses and communication.

10. Break down unspecified verbal maps into higher quality verbal descriptions and, more importantly, behavioral demonstrations and examples to create easily shared and observable representations of the client's experiences and outcomes.

11. Frame and re-frame problematic behaviors and responses and make explicit the positive intentions and positive by-products underlying them. The purpose of this is to create a shift in the perceptions of family members, with respect to the behavior, so

that it may be handled more resourcefully. The shift in perception functions to:

a. separate "self" from "behavior" through the reinforcement and validation of the individual as a person by associating the "self" with the positive intent. Any negative responses may, then, be directed toward the behavioral manifestation and not the person himself.

b. preserve the positive intent of the problematic behavior even though the behavioral means used to secure the positive intention are altered.

c. preserve and validate the positive by-product of the behavior or response, which serves to help preserve the ecology of the family system as well as, again, validate the "self" while changing the unwanted behavior.

12. Create and reinforce flexibility in family members through role playing and other forms of behavioral modeling, to help family members more consistently and systematically elicit desired behaviors and responses in other family members.

13. Eliciting and detailing a high quality description and demonstration of the client's desired state(s) that will be well-formed, practical, and ecological for the particular family system.

These techniques, as stated, have been briefly discussed, and it would be neither useful nor practical to present them all in full detail. This is especially so since we are communicating through written language which, by virtue of the medium itself, contains none of the tremendous amount of sensory experience that is only available in a seminar, workshop, or credentialing program. Given these limitations, however, we would like to present a few of the basic techniques in more detail in this section. Specifically, we will present some basic *anchoring* and *reframing* techniques, some guidelines to setting up and installing self-reinforcing *calibrated loops,* and *future-pacing.* As you read on, and plan how to utilize these techniques in your work, however, it will be very important to keep in mind that the use of each technique we are describing presupposes that the therapist has *already* established rapport with the client(s) and has identified and detailed a well-formed and ecological outcome.

Anchoring

Anchoring is a technique used to re-program and re-sequence responses of family members. As mentioned previously, anchoring is the learned association between a stimulus and a response, or between one response and another. When the stimulus, or initiating response, is triggered, the associated response will be elicited.

There are several skills that are required of the therapist in the use of anchoring. The first is the ability to elicit responses in clients. This can be accomplished, as mentioned previously, by doing the following: having clients remember a time in the past when they had the same response; doing something to elicit the response you want to anchor in the ongoing context; by having clients imagine a time in the future when they know they will or think they might have the response; or to have clients think of someone else who has the response, and act as if they were that person. It is extremely important that the therapist be expressive in his vocal qualities and gestures in helping clients access resources. "The more expressive you are, the more expressiveness you are apt to elicit, and your own behaviors need to be congruent with the response you are asking for." (Cameron-Bandler, 1978, p. 104)

The second skill required in anchoring is the therapist's ability to detect, visually and auditorally, when the response in the client is beginning to be elicited, reaches peak intensity, and declines in intensity. Such sensory experience is necessary because the response must be anchored when it peaks. The anchor that the therapist uses can be any external stimulus, such as a touch, a particular voice tone, a gesture, or a snap of the fingers. We have found that kinesthetic anchors (a specific touch on the client's knee, arm, shoulder, etc.) are the least difficult for the novice to learn.

The therapist must also have the skills to recapitulate the anchor. If a touch anchor is used, the therapist must reproduce that anchor in the exact location, and with the exact pressure, that was used when the anchor was established, in order to elicit the maximum response from the client.

Anchoring can be used to change previously existing anchors in the family system that have produced unwanted responses. The anchors involved in recursive sequences of external behaviors and internal responses that we label "calibrated loops" are examples of these. This is accomplished by changing a family member's unwanted, internal response to the anchor of another family member's external behavior into a more useful or desired response.

One of the authors worked with a couple who were anchored in the following calibrated loop. In the middle of a conversation with his wife, the husband would pause, shake his head, and sigh. This behavior would elicit an internal response in his wife (which she later labelled "irritation") that would produce a "harshness" in her tonality, and a rise in volume in her next verbalization to her husband. This behavior would elicit an internal response in him (which he labelled "anger") producing a reddening of his skin color, another pause, shake of the head, and a deeper sigh, which elicited in her a more intense response of "irritation." This loop would continue until the couple was arguing intensely.

The most useful point of intervention in this loop is the first response of irritation elicited by the husband's first pause, shake of the head, and sigh. The first task of the therapist is to test the assumed association between the external behavior and the ensuing internal response. The therapist did this by using the pattern we in NLP call "quotes" (Bandler and Grinder, 1975). Quotes is a pattern in which a message that you want to deliver can be embedded in quotations, as if someone else had stated the message. The purpose of this pattern is to allow you to deliver messages so that the response to that message will not be attached to you, but to the statement or behavior in quotes. You, as therapist, do not want negative responses attached or anchored to you. Thus, the therapist in the above example said to the wife:

> Your husband reminds me very much of a client I once had. The first time I saw the client he said to me, *"You know I really think that (pause, shake of the head, and sigh) my wife doesn't love me anymore."*

Applications of Neuro-Linguistic Programming

After saying the above, the therapist saw and heard that the same set of minimal cues associated with "irritation," and indeed, the wife's next verbalization to the therapist was characterized by the same harshness in tonality and rise in volume. The test was thus positive.

If the therapist in the above example had not recapitulated the husband's behavior in quotes, there is a possibility that the wife would attach the same negative response to the therapist as she does to her husband. This, of course, needs to be avoided. Indeed, many therapists, in conversations with clients, attach negative responses to themselves without knowing it.

The programmer's next step was to explain to the couple the principle of a calibrated loop, and the sequence of behaviors and responses that characterized the calibrated loop in which they were involved. After securing the desire on the part of the couple to change this, the therapist asked the wife to recall that her husband would pause, shake his head, and sigh, and to imagine what *she* would be experiencing on the inside if *she* were doing that. The wife responded that she would probably feel pretty frustrated. The programmer then asked the wife how *she* would like to be responded to if she were acting in the way her husband did, and feeling frustrated. She indicated that she would like the other person to recognize that she was doing the best that she could, to try to support her, and help her. She was then asked if she would want the other person to talk harshly to her, if that person was trying to help. She said that, on the contrary, the person should speak softly and gently. The wife was then directed to recall a time when she recognized the many difficulties her husband found in his work or in other areas, realized that he was doing his best, and really wanted to help the best that she could. As she accessed this response, an associated set of behavioral cues, which included soft voice qualities, was noticed by the therapist. At the peak of expression of this response, the wife was anchored kinesthetically, by a touch on her shoulder. The establishment of the anchor was tested by triggering it and noticing that the same set of behavioral cues was elicited.

The therapist then directed the husband to repeat his behavior, and as he did so the therapist triggered the anchor on the wife's shoulder. This process was repeated several times. Each time the anchor was triggered, the therapist noticed the same set of behavioral cues associated with the response of desire to help her husband as best she could. Finally, without triggering the anchor, the therapist directed the husband to repeat his behavior. Once again, the same set of new cues was elicited. Thus the husband's pause, shake of the head, and sigh were now an anchor for the response of a desire to help in his wife. The problematic loop was broken and a more useful one established.

The steps to follow, in changing the internal response to an external behavior using anchoring, are as follows:

1. Test the external behavior/internal response association by recapitulating the behavior in quotes, or through a metaphor, and notice if the same response is elicited.

2. Determine an internal response that would be more useful and worthwhile to have than the cur-

rent one. Access and calibrate (notice what set of minimal cues are associated with the response).

3. Anchor the response and test the establishment of the anchor.

4. Have a family member recapitulate the external behavior, and trigger the anchor in the other family member. Repeat several times, noticing if the set of minimal cues associated with the new response is elicited.

5. Repeat step 4 above, without the anchor.

6. If at any time during steps 3, 4, and 5 the set of minimal cues associated with the new response are not elicited, return to step 2.

Reframing

Reframing is a second set of techniques that we use in family therapy. We will discuss *content* and *context* reframing (Cameron-Bandler, 1978) in the context of working with families. As we mentioned earlier, the purpose of reframing is to shift the perceptions of family members with respect to another family member's external behavior so that these perceptions may be more resourcefully handled.

In a *content reframe,* the therapist attaches a positive intent to a family member's external behavior that elicits a negative response in another family member. This effectively shifts the internal responses to that behavior. A teenage son, in a family that one of the authors was treating, complained that his father always objected to any future plans that he, the young man, discussed. The therapist said to the teenager, "Isn't it nice to have a father who doesn't want you to be hurt or disappointed in any way? I'll bet you don't know very many fathers who care that much about their children." This statement was enough to shift the teenager's internal response to his father's objections from one of anger only to one that included sincere appreciation. This new framing of the father's behavior allowed the youth to consider his father a resource for helping him learn how to plan his future, rather than as a liability or roadblock. The validation of the father's intent also allowed the father to shift his perception of his own role (and thus his method of participation) in his son's life to one that was primarily supportive as opposed to primarily inhibitory.

The format for generating content reframes is as follows:

1. Pick a behavior of one family member that elicits a negative response in another family member or members.

2. Determine a possible positive intention that could underlie that behavior. There are two aspects to the intent. The first is a positive internal response behind the behavior, (for example, love, caring, and respect). The second is the positive benefit the behavior could accomplish for the other family member.

3. Pair the positive internal response with the positive benefit in a rhetorical question of the form, "Do you realize. . . . ?" or, "Isn't it nice. . . . ?", as in the example above.

Perhaps one of the most powerful content reframes the programmer can offer to a family is to teach them about representational systems. Not only does this allow the family members to perceive and respond to each other at a new level of awareness, but it gives them the realization that other members have *not* been behaving in a problematic fashion or mis-communicating out of malice, or hate, or anger, but rather because they are more visually, auditorily, or kinesthetically oriented.

According to Cameron-Bandler (1978) *contextual reframing* "accepts all behaviors as useful in some context" (p. 131). The purpose of contextual reframing is, once again, to change a family member's negative internal response to another family member's external behavior. This is accomplished by having the first family member realize the usefulness of the behavior in some contexts.

One of the authors worked with a family in which a teenage son was constantly getting into fights at school (which he usually won). The mother was outraged at his behavior. The therapist said to her, "Isn't it nice to know that John could protect Wendy (his 14-year-old sister) if anyone attacked her on the way home from school?" Again, this was enough to shift her response to her son's behavior. Rather than being outraged, now the mother could appreciate her son's behavior as useful in a particular context. As anyone who has worked with families knows, negative responses often serve to maintain and even escalate problematic behaviors, rather than extinguish them. The mother's new choice, to respond positively to her son's behavior in a single context, gives her a resource to more usefully communicate with her son about his behavior. Having his own behavior validated as useful in a particular context, rather than being attacked and criticized, the son is also allowed to view his own behavior from a different perspective, rather than constantly being on the defensive.

A next step with the mother and son, of course, is to establish the positive intent and positive by-products that John gets from the behavior and find some more appropriate substitutes.

The steps in a contextual reframe are:

1. Pick a behavior of family member A that elicits a negative response in family member B.

2. Find a context in which this behavior might elicit a positive response in family member B.

3. Ask a rhetorical question in which the behavior is put in positive context.

Establishing a Self-Reinforcing Loop

We call the third technique *establishing a self-reinforcing loop*. One of the most important goals of the family therapist is to get desired changes to persist when the therapist is not there to supervise or help with the family's interactions. Many therapists attempt to do this by establishing contracts, or agreements, between family members. Most often, however, the motivation to fulfill the contract is external to the changes in behavior being agreed to, and the behaviors themselves are not self-reinforcing. The carrying out of the contract, then, becomes another chore, or responsibility, that can be detrimental to the client's motivation to follow through.

In Neuro-Linguistic Programming, we accomplish the above therapeutic goal by establishing a positive calibrated loop between family members that is self-reinforcing. Rather than making contracts, or agreements, between family members, where each

Applications of Neuro-Linguistic Programming

member is responsible for the agreed-upon changes in behavior with which each member may or may not be happy, the responsibility for any behavioral change is put into the hands of the member(s) who desires it. The technique we use is drawn from the presupposition that the meaning of any communication is the response it elicits. When one family member systematically fails to respond to a request from another, one can just as easily frame that failure as a result of a lack of flexibility on the part of the family member who desires the change to elicit the response he or she intends to elicit. To set up a positive self-reinforcing calibrated loop, we have each family member who desires a change in another family member find out what they would need to do in order to make the other family member *want* to change his behavior or responses. As a simple example, imagine you are working with a husband and wife. The husband wants to have the house clean and dinner ready when he arrives home from work. The wife wants her husband to make love to her more often. Rather than make a contract, or agreement, that each will do their part, the programmer will have the wife ask the husband, "What could I do that would make you *want* to make love with me more often?" or, "what would compel you to *want* to make love with me more often?" Likewise, the programmer will have the husband ask, "What can I do to get you to *want* to have the house clean and dinner ready?" Once the behavior is identified that is necessary to get the person to respond the way the other party desires, a reinforcing loop can be set up. The motivation for each party to produce the behavior that will make the other party want to respond is the fact that each desires the response by definition.

Many times you will find that the activities that would make each party want to respond will be related. In the above example, the wife may tell the husband that if he entertained guests at home more often, she would take pride in the house and want to keep it clean. The husband may tell the wife that if she dressed up more often, took better care of her appearance, and looked more attractive, he would want to make love with her more often. These can be linked together in that if they entertained more at home the wife would dress up and take better care of the house. Thus, a full loop may be established.

Sometimes, the behaviors desired from each party can be directly linked together to form the positively reinforcing loop. For instance, if the husband came home and found the house was less cluttered and dinner ready, he may be more relaxed and at ease, and more in touch with his feelings. By being more in touch with his feelings, he may become sexually aroused more easily, and more sexually active with his wife. The wife, happy with the response from her husband, may want to make the house look nice for him, have dinner ready on time, and so on. Each loop will be tailored, of course, to fit the unique individuals involved.

The following format is a step-by-step procedure you can use to help generate positively reinforcing loops:

1. Have family member A pick a behavior that they want to be able to get family member B to do.

2. Have A ask, "What are three things I could do to get you to *want* to do_____for me?"

3. Secure an agreement from A that he is willing to do those three things. If he is not willing, go back to step 2.

4. Switch

Futurepacing

Futurepacing is another technique used in NLP to insure that desired outcomes and resources persist outside of the therapeutic context. For a discussion of this technique, we quote Cameron-Bandler (1978):

> Essentially futurepacing refers to the process of insuring that the changes accomplished during therapy become generalized and available in the appropriate outside contexts. Too often, changes that occur in therapy become anchored to the therapist's office or even to the therapist himself, rather than being available to the client in the specific situations that most need the new behaviors and responses.
> The primary method of futurepacing new behaviors is by anchoring the new behavior or response to a sensory stimulus that naturally occurs in the applicable context. . . .
> Futurepacing can be done very directly. One way is to ask the client, "What is the very first thing you will see, hear, or feel externally that will indicate that you need this resource?" When the specific experience is identified, have the client generate it internally and then anchor it to the appropriate resource. Then, when the stimulus occurs in external experience it can naturally or unconsciously trigger the appropriate feelings/behavior. For instance, anchoring feelings of passion (the resource) to the feeling of smooth, cool sheets or the sound of his name softly whispered, or the sight of a yellow rose, is futurepacing the resource of passionate feelings to specific externally occurring experiences.
> Futurepacing is not frosting on the therapy cake. Without adequate futurepacing, the accomplishments of a session are often lost. It is the final step in any therapeutic intervention. (pp. 159–160)

We have welcomed the opportunity to present in some detail a few of the techniques we use in working with families. Other techniques, available through our seminars or in our books, that we use include *hypnotic language patterns* (Bandler and Grinder, 1976), *therapeutic metaphors,* in which a therapist can embed any therapeutic technique in a story, fairy tale, and so on (Gordon, 1978), *elicitation* and *utilization of strategies* (Dilts, et al., 1980), *change personal history,* a technique designed to change a client's subjective experience of past, painful events (Cameron-Bandler, 1978), and *six-step reframing,* a technique developed to deal with problems, such as habits or medical problems, in which there is secondary gain involved (Cameron-Bandler, 1978, Bandler and Grinder, 1979). We trust that the reader will consult these reference sources for more information on these valuable and useful techniques.

We want to assure the reader that all of these techniques are used in conjunction with others. We demand of our students that they select, sequence, and modify techniques to secure the desired outcomes of family members. We make this demand because any imposed restrictions in selection, sequencing, and modification of techniques impose limitations on the flexibility of the therapist, and would thus limit the therapist's ability to help clients get desired outcomes in therapy. No technique is a substitute for the ability to 1) set an explicit trajectory toward an outcome, 2) have open, active sensory experience, and 3) have a wide-ranging flexibility of internal responses and external behaviors to achieve those outcomes.

CASE EXAMPLE

A family of four spent a total of four sessions in therapy with one of the authors. The family consisted of the parents, Bob and Jean, a couple in their early forties, a fifteen-year-old son, Doug, and a ten-year-old daughter, Terry.

The first session involved the initial establishment of rapport by matching predicates and body posture in each family member. It was discovered that the father was highly specialized in his use of kinesthetic predicates, the mother and son, auditory predicates and the daughter, visual. Their initial complaints were that the son was alcoholic, and the parents argued constantly about what to do with him. It was decided, with agreement from the family, to see the son in individual therapy, initially, to see the parents as a couple concurrently, and later to see the family as a unit. The rest of the initial session was spent with the parents.

The following is a portion of the ensuing dialogue with the parents. Please remember that the transcript is only a minimal portion of all that was occurring. It is only a presentation of the linguistic interactions. Keep in mind that, as the therapist is talking to each person, he is maintaining rapport nonverbally by adjusting his posture and tonality to match the individual he is communicating with.

T. Bob, I'm curious about what it is that you want for yourself. (establishment of outcome)

B. Well, I feel that we really need some changes in our relationship.

T. What changes, specifically? (meta model question)

B. Well, lately, I just haven't been able to get a handle on where Jean is. I guess I'd just like to feel more love from her.

T. Bob, how do you know when Jean is loving you more? (complex equivalence question)

B. When she touches me. She hasn't been doing as much of that lately as she used to.

T. Could you demonstrate to Jean how, specifically, you would like her to touch you? (Bob does so)

T. Good. Bob, I'm wondering what it was like for you in the past when Jean touched you that way.

B. (Therapist notices Bob's facial muscles relaxing, breathing rate increasing, skin color reddening, and other changes in minimal cues as Bob accesses this state.) It was wonderful. (As response peaks therapist anchors it.)

T. Good. Bob, I'll let you hang on to that feeling while I talk to Jean. Jean, what, specifically, do you want from Bob? (outcome question)

J. I just want him to respect me.

T. I'm wondering how you know when Bob does respect you. (complex equivalence question)

J. He listens to me and doesn't interrupt me when I'm talking.

T. Does he *always* interrupt you now? (counter example)

J. No, just when I'm trying to discipline the children.

Applications of Neuro-Linguistic Programming

T. How, specifically, does he interrupt you? (complex equivalence)

J. I'll be talking to the kids about something they've done and he'll just walk right in between the kids and me and start yelling at them. Then I just don't think he respects my abilities as a parent.

T. He loves you so much that he gets angry when the kids upset you. (content reframe)

J. What?

T. I said that he interrupts you and yells at the kids because he loves you so much he gets angry when the kids upset you.

J. I never thought of it that way. (Therapist notices changes in minimal cues associated with this verbalization.)

T. Jean, what do you want Bob to do when you're disciplining the children? (Outcome)

J. I'd like him to just stay in the background. If I need him I'll call him.

B. But I'm just trying to help you handle the situation.

T. Bob, I want you to realize that when you interrupt Jean when she's talking to the kids, it's like having someone rubbing their hands gently over your face, then without warning, slapping you. (translation of auditory experience to kinesthetic)

B. Gee, I never realized what an impact that caused.

T. Bob, what are three things Jean could do to get you to *want* to stop interrupting her? (setting up positive loop.)

B. Well, if it makes her feel that bad, of course, I want to stop doing it. But, I guess she could tell me later what the kids did and how she disciplined them.

T. Two other things.

B. Well, she could call me if she needed assistance, particularly if it was something that Doug did that was best dealt with by a father. You know, dating and sex.

T. And a third one?

B. Well, if it was something where she was hurt, rather than angry, I'd want to do the disciplining.

T. Jean, are you willing to agree to those conditions?

J. Yes.

T. Bob, you want Jean to touch you more often. (Therapist triggers anchor and the set of minimal cues associated with the anchor are elicited.)

B. Yes.

T. I want you to ask Jean what are three things that you could do to get her to want to touch you more often. (set up positive loop)

B. (Repeats the question.)

J. Well, the first thing you could do is to tell me when you want to be touched. The second is to touch me first. And the third I guess is to tell me that you love me, that's like a touch for me.

T. Jean, I want you to hear that you just told Bob about your experience in words that he could understand. You translated your auditory experience of knowing that you're loved into a kinesthetic one that Bob could understand... Now Bob, are you willing to do those things?

B. Yes.

The rest of the session was spent clarifying other desired outcomes that the parents had.

During the next session with Bob and Jean the outcome that was achieved was for them to be able to elicit desired sexual responses from each other. During the past fifteen years of marriage each had one brief affair which was for each "just a sex thing." When asked how he tried to "turn his wife on," Bob stated, "I just begin touching her." Upon being queried about her response to this behavior, Jean replied, "He never listens. For fifteen years I've told him that when he just begins by touching me that I sometimes feel manhandled. It turns me off."

When asked to demonstrate how she tried to turn Bob on, Jean began to talk to him in a breathy whisper about what she wanted him to do to her. In response to this he burst out laughing, stating that for fifteen years he found that behavior to be silly and clichéd, like a movie. Jean responded, "It makes me so mad that he laughs at me, so I've just given up trying to turn him on."

A positive reinforcing loop was set up, with the result that Jean wanted Bob to talk to her in a low tone, slow tempo, breathy voice before he touched her in order for him to elicit a strong sexual response from her. Bob, on the other hand, wanted his wife to touch him in "special ways," which he demonstrated to her. As we've often found in families, Bob was trying to elicit a response in Jean the way he wanted Jean to elicit that response in him, and vice versa. The meaning of Bob and Jean's communication was the response that they got, and not what each intended.

The third and fourth sessions were spent with the entire family discussing what responses the children wanted to be able to elicit in their parents and vice versa. In working with Doug individually, the therapist discovered that a positive by-product of Doug's drinking was that, in an inebriated state of consciousness, he felt "confident." When asked what in the family system prevented Doug from being confident without drinking, he reported, "Dad does everything really well. He always tells me what I'm doing wrong." It was then established that the father's positive intent was to help Doug "learn." His behavior, however, achieved the opposite. What Doug needed in order to be able to learn was to be confident.

When asked what his dad could do to make him feel more "confident," Doug replied, "Just tell me how well I'm doing, rather than how bad." Bob agreed, but the author noticed a slight unconscious shaking of Bob's head from side to side as he said he would do what his son asked. The author pointed out the multiple messages and asked Bob if he was fully congruent with his responses. Bob said that he really wanted to help his son by only telling him how well he'd done, but that some feedback was a necessary part of learning. Doug was then asked what his father could do to give him feedback and still make him feel confident. It was agreed that any feedback given to Doug was to follow a statement of what Doug had done well already and that any such advice was to be stated in positive terms. That is, what could be done as an improvement, as opposed to what was wrong.

Terry, the daughter, wanted to see that everyone was getting along better. After seeing the changes in everyone during the session, she felt confident that things were well on their way and didn't need any special attention.

To help the parents elicit desired behaviors from the children, such as cleaning their rooms, the therapist used the opportunity to instill in the family an explicit way of setting up their own reinforcing loops.

A measure of success of the four sessions was a phone call the therapist received from Bob two months later. Bob reported that several other problems had arisen in the three months time, but that the family had been able to solve them themselves with the techniques they had learned. The therapist talked to each family member in turn and discovered, indeed, that each was able to get desired responses from other family members.

SUMMARY

As we have stated, we believe that the outcome, in family therapy, is for family members to be able to elicit desired internal and external behavioral responses from one another in a way that does not jeopardize the ecology of the family system. To achieve this outcome it is minimally necessary for both the therapist and the family to adopt into their behavior the three NLP presuppositions that are most important in family therapy. These presuppositions are: 1) the meaning of any communication is the response it elicits; 2) there is no substitute in communications for using the sensory experience to know what response is being elicited by your behavior; and 3) if you are not getting the response you want, employ the principle of flexibility or try another behavior to get the desired response. To the family members, adopting these presuppositions will insure that they can get the responses they want. The therapist who adopts these presuppositions will find that there are no more "resistant" clients and that outcomes for clients are achieved more effectively and quickly.

The patterns and techniques we have presented here are only maps. We have found these maps useful and effective for charting the present state and desired state of family systems and evolving the family system from the former to the latter. Again, we caution the reader that "the map is not the territory." We would hope that the therapists we train do what works, rather than following maps that may not be useful. A map of California will not help you find your way from New York City to Paris, France. However, we hope that the maps that we have introduced to you may assist you in finding your way toward desired professional and personal outcomes.

Our outcome in writing this chapter was to provide the reader with an introduction to the family therapy applications of Neuro-Linguistic Programming™. We want to assure the reader that what we have presented here is only a limited representation of the overall model of NLP in family therapy. We hope that our discussions here have whetted the reader's appetite for more. We encourage you to read some of the NLP references cited in this work for a fuller explanation of the material we have presented here. Since we believe that the highest quality of information is behavioral, we also encourage you to attend an NLP seminar where the richness of direct experience will be offered to you.

EVALUATION AND RESEARCH

In researching a particular theory or model there are two directions that may be taken: 1) evaluating the truthfulness of the model's claims, or 2) evaluating the usefulness of the model's claims. Since NLP is truly an outcome-oriented model and since the basic presupposition on which the entire model was developed is that the map is not the territory, it should not be necessary to explain to the reader why the first of these two directions is of little interest to the Neuro-Linguistic Programmer. Research that attempts to evaluate the truthfulness of a model's claims generally does so on the basis of statistical averaging and other statistical computations. Because NLP is concerned with the identification and utilization of behavioral *patterns* in an ongoing interaction, statistical quantities are of no value to us. Surely, a statistical figure tells nothing of the unique individual(s) before you. In NLP we believe that people have to rely on statistics when they *don't* understand the underlying pattern.

There have, naturally, been a number of studies validating some of the fundamental tenets of the NLP model such as: eye movements as indicators of representational access; commonly used sensory-based predicates as indicators of preferred representational system; the positive effects on clients of pacing their predicates. There has even been research correlating preferred representational system with base line EEG brain wave patterns.

In terms of evaluating the usefulness of the model's claims, NLP is in somewhat of a unique position, as usefulness is the primary criterion for including a pattern in the model to begin with. In many ways the development of NLP has been the result of one major, ongoing research project to extract those patterns that were and are useful from people who were the masters of their craft. NLP was developed by researching what people *did* who were already world renowned for their abilities to achieve outcomes in their chosen field. Yet, surely, as more patterns are added to the NLP technology and as the scope of its applications broadens it must be continually tested and evaluated.

One difficulty we have found in the research style of people (other than the developers or highly trained practitioners) who have tried to evaluate the effectiveness of NLP techniques is that their methodology generally attempts to isolate one piece or portion of the model and examine it as an independent pattern. Anyone who has experience with NLP, or with therapy in general for that matter, will know that it is impossible to assess the effects of anchoring or reframing outside of the concomitant impact of the degree of rapport between client and therapist, or vice versa. Similarly it is impossible to quantify the effects of pacing predicates independent of the effects of the nonverbal interaction. The various patterns that make up the body of NLP were isolated and made explicit, as separate pieces, in order to make them easily learnable. In order to make them useful, however, they must be applied simultaneously, as a whole.

The Society of Neuro-Linguistic Programming was established as a solution to the difficulties experienced by many of those who attempted to research and evaluate NLP. Organized and staffed by the developers and foremost trainers and practitioners of NLP, this organization is coordinating information on research projects involving the applications of NLP in many areas. Projects include applications of NLP to the treatment of phobias; to smoking and weight control; to the treatment of learning disabilities; to the treatment of psychosomatic illness and cancer; to the enhancement of creativity and accelerated learning as well as computer assisted learning; and to the effectiveness of NLP in business management and sales. Although the experimental format will vary, most of the projects involve a series of single case experiments (see Hersen and Barlow, 1976), and records consisting of videotaped sessions rather than forms and numbers.

Neuro-Linguistic Programming is a young field. And, since the Society has been established only recently, the results of many of these projects are not available at the time of this writing. The Society, however, does maintain an updated listing of completed research projects, dissertations, and so forth, on NLP and NLP-related material. If you are interested in obtaining a listing of completed research, participating in ongoing research, or proposing a research topic please write to:

> NLP Research
> P.O. Box 67448
> Scotts Valley CA 95067

SUGGESTED READINGS

Frogs Into Princes contains edited transcripts of a three-day introductory seminar conducted by Richard Bandler and John Grinder. It is an entertaining and highly readable book that will provide the reader with an excellent introduction to Neuro-Linguistic Programming.

They Lived Happily Ever After, authored by Leslie Cameron-Bandler, is a book about the application of the basic patterns of NLP to couples and sex therapy. Many of the basic techniques of NLP, such as anchoring, change personal history, visual-kinesthetic disassociation, and 6-step reframing are presented in a step-by-step format with case examples illustrating their use in therapy.

Neuro-Linguistic Programming, Volume I, by Robert Dilts, John Grinder, Richard Bandler, Leslie Cameron-Bandler, and Judith DeLozier, is the fundamental book about the cognitive processes that underlie all behavior—strategies. Truly a renaissance work in the behavioral sciences, this book will reveal to the reader why Neuro-Linguistic Programming can be considered a new scientific discipline.

The *Structure of Magic I,* by Richard Bandler and John Grinder, is a book about linguistic phenomena in therapy. It contains the meta model, a model of information gathering that will present to the reader an explicit method of identifying linguistic violations in the client's language, and a set of questions designed to recover the missing pieces in a client's verbalizations. The meta model allows both the client and the therapist to discover information about the client's experience of the world, information that is often hidden in language.

Changing with Families, by Richard Bandler, John Grinder, and Virginia Satir contains patterns and techniques derived from Bandler's and Grinder's modeling of Virginia Satir's remarkable work with families. Much of the fundamental information about the meta model, representational systems, and calibrated loops in family systems that forms the foundation for the NLP in family therapy model is included.

Patterns of the Hypnotic Techniques of Milton H. Erickson, M.D. Vol. I, by Richard Bandler and John Grinder presents the reader with an explicit model derived from Erickson's work on the use of hypnotic language patterning in therapy. The use of such language patterns in therapy provides the therapist with greater flexibility and the reduction of resistance from clients that may be elicited by the therapist's typical language style.

AUTHORS

Robert Dilts is the President of Behavioral Engineering, a company that produces computer software incorporating the principles of Neuro-Linguistic Programming. He is the major contributing author of *Neuro-Linguistic Programming, Volume I,* and is the author of several monographs on NLP, "Neuro-Linguistic Programming: A New Psychotherapy," "Neuro-Linguistic Programming in Education," "Neuro-Linguistic Programming in Organizational Development," and "EEG and Representational Systems."

He has been working with and teaching the communication tools of NLP since 1975 when it was first being formalized as a behavioral model. In the past six years he has contributed to the development of many of the basic concepts of the model. He has also conducted and been actively involved in the clinical and experimental research supporting many of the basic tenets of NLP, including research conducted at Langley-Porter Neuropsychiatric Institute.

He is currently designing and conducting research to discover and support new patterns and principles of human communication, as well as teaching NLP seminars nationwide.

David Green received his Ph.D. from Indiana State University in 1979. He is a Certified Trainer in NLP and served as an associate staff member of Not Ltd.'s Division of Training and Research. He has taught NLP seminars nationwide to psychotherapists, social workers, salespeople, managers, police, law enforcement, and corrections officers. He is the author of several articles on NLP and is currently in private practice in Los Angeles.

REFERENCES

Ashby, W., Ross: *An Introduction to Cybernetics.* London, Methuen and Co, 1964.

Bandler, R., Grinder, J.: *Frogs into Princes.* Moab, Utah, Real People Press, 1979.

Bandler, R., Grinder, J.: *The Structure of Magic I.* Palo Alto, CA, Science and Behavior Books, 1975.

Bandler, R., Grinder, J.: *Patterns of the Hypnotic Techniques of Milton H. Erickson, M.D., Vol. I.* Cupertino, CA, Meta Publications, 1975.

Bandler, R., Grinder, J., Satir, V.: *Changing With Families,* Palo Alto, CA, Science and Behavior Books, 1976.

Bateson, G.: *Steps to an Ecology of Mind.* New York, Ballantine Books, 1972.

Cameron-Bandler. L.: *They Lived Happily Ever After.* Cupertino, CA, Meta Publications, 1978.

Dilts, R., Grinder, J., Bandler, R., Cameron-Bandler, L., DeLozier, J.: *Neuro-Linguistic Programming, Vol. I.* Cupertino, CA, Meta Publications, 1980.

Erickson, M.: *Advanced Techniques of Hypnosis and Therapy* (Haley J, Ed.). New York, Grune and Stratton, 1967.

Gordon, D.: *Therapeutic Metaphors.* Cupertino, CA, Meta Publications, 1978.

Green, D.: "Nominalization in Couple Counseling", *The Journal for Specialists in Group Work* 4(2), 75–79, 1979.

Grinder, J., Bandler, R.: *The Structure of Magic II.* Palo Alto, CA, Science and Behavior Books, 1976.

Grinder, J., DeLozier, J., Bandler, R.: *Patterns of the Hypnotic Techniques of Milton H. Erickson, M.D., Vol. II.* Cupertino, CA, Meta Publications, 1977.

Haley, J.: *Uncommon Therapy.* New York, W. W. Norton and Co., 1973.

Hersen, M., Barlow, D.: *Single Case Experimental Designs.* New York, Pergamon Press, 1976.

Laing, R. D., Esterson, A.: *Sanity, Madness and the Family.* London: Tavistock Publications, 1964.

Satir, V.: *Peoplemaking.* Palo Alto, CA, Science and Behavior Books, 1972.

THE META MODEL LIVE

BY ROBERT B. DILTS

(1979)

TABLE OF CONTENTS

PART	PAGE
I. Introduction	3
Development of the Meta Model	6
A. Deletions	8
1. Comparatives and Superlatives	9
B. Unspecified Referential Index	10
C. Nominalizations	11
1. Transderivational Search	13
D. Unspecified Verbs	16
E. Modal Operators	17
F. Presuppositions	19
G. Cause-Effect	19
H. Universal Quantifiers	20
1. Sensory Experience	21
2. Rapport	23
I. Lost Performatives	23
J. Mind Reading	24
K. Complex Equivalence	25
III. Comments on the Use of the Meta Model	27
IV. Organizing Meta Model Questions	30
A. Algorithm For Change	31
1. Therapist's Syndrome	32
B. Establishing Desired States	33
C. Eleciting Resources	36
D. Goals of the Meta Model	37

I. INTRODUCTION

Learning the Meta Model is essentially learning how to hear and identify patterns in people's language.

I'll present the patterns and talk a little about them and then we'll break up into groups and practice them.

The Meta Model is probably one of the most important things to learn as a professional communicator because it is a way to gather high-quality information from the people that you are working with, no matter what kind of field you are in.

I will start with a story about gathering information and the Meta Model:

I was up in Canada doing a workshop on hypnosis with a group of people and there was a gentleman there who was a hypnotist. He told us a story that was very interesting. He said that at one time he had this woman come in as a client. He sat her down and he did some hypnotic tests. She seemed to be a good subject and he had good rapport with her. He started off doing this induction, with his most refined Ericsonian techniques, using tonal markings, embedded commands, and all those various things. After about half an hour she was still sitting there with her eyes open and nothing was happening. He finally stopped and said, "Gee, I don't understand what is going on. You seem to have good susceptibility, and there seems to be good rapport. I can't find any reason for it, but you don't seem to go into a trance very easily. Is everything alright?" So, she says to him, "Well, you haven't shown me one of those things yet." He asks, "What things?" and she says, "You know, the crystal ball." He says to himself, "That's one of those pieces of archaic paraphernalia that old-time hypnotists used," but he thinks he has one back in his drawer that he used to use for stage demonstrations. So he goes rummaging through his bottom drawer.

He reaches way in the back of the drawer and pulls out this pendulum sort of thing, and he says, "You mean this?" and holds it up. She goes, "Yes," and collapses immediately into a deep trance . . . (Laughter).

I had an experience that was very much like that when I was working with a woman on weight control. I elicited her strategy and tried to program in a new strategy using anchoring and stuff like that. I thought I did a nice job, but she came back a week later and says, "Well, it worked a little bit, but I am still not having much success." I couldn't figure it out. Finally, I asked her if she had ever changed a problematic behavior before. And she said, "Well, I was sort of expecting that you would do this thing that this dentist did to me once." I said, "And what, specifically, was that?" And she goes on to tell me the story about how she used to be so nervous going to the dentist's office until one day the dentist got frustrated trying to work on her, and said, "I'll have to do hypnosis with you!" She said he just grabbed on to her wrist and told her over and over how she would be comfortable the next time she came in. And she said, "I didn't go into a deep trance or anything like that, but I was sure surprised the next time I came in. I wasn't nervous at all." So, after I talked to her for a while, I just reached down and said the exact same thing he did. I used the same kind of intonation she used when imitating her dentist. I held her wrist and said, over and over, "You will have no trouble with your eating patterns this week and will lose weight comfortably." Then I told her that she'd just been in a hypnotic trance that would cure her weight problem, and to go home and call me in a week. She called back a week later and said, "Wow, this is great. This is just what I wanted. I've lost eight pounds already." The point is that I tried doing various techniques with little success until I asked for the information I needed. Then, she literally told me what I needed to do in order to make a change, because she had a reference experience.

Now, for me, this is what the Meta Model is all about: being able to increase your efficiency in anything by finding out that kind of specific information. Knowing anchoring, knowing strategies, or any technique by itself isn't going to get you anywhere unless you know *how* and *when* to use them. I could have done my best piece of strategy work with this woman, but there was something else that she wanted, one thing that she needed before she was willing to respond, just like the lady who was working with the hypnotist. For me, the Meta Model is all about asking these kinds of questions. What do you need? What would happen if you did? And that kind of stuff.

II. Development of the Meta Model

For those of you who haven't had experience with it before, I would like to start off from the beginning and take you down through the Meta Model ages.

It was first developed by John Grinder and Richard Bandler. In fact, this was the very first thing that they developed together. All the rest of NLP was discovered and developed by asking these questions. So this should be a good motivation for you. While there are other techniques, everything was precipitated by the Meta Model—which is simply asking questions. It is simply gathering information and questioning.

John and Richard started by studying Virginia Satir and Fritz Perls. In trying to find out what these therapeutic wizards did, they noticed that these therapists asked certain kinds of questions. Now, John was a linguist. He had all these neat categories in his head. He had studied this kind of stuff in college. But they were basically just academic things for him. Then he got together with Richard, and they put together this model that applied linguistic knowledge to actual behavior.

It is all based on the idea that *the map is not the territory.*

In order to operate on the world we all make maps of what is going on out there with our sensory apparatus, our eyes, ears, noses, mouths, and bodies. We also make maps of those maps, or models of those models, with our language systems. We call this a Meta Model, a model about modeling.

Now, we do this mapping with language, in other words, we map out our experience through language. Words are anchors for experience. A word is as much an anchor as a squeeze on the knee. Words tend to be the most common anchoring system, because there are so many changes that you can make in tonal qualities and the various phonological things that you can do with your mouth and lips. So it is a very refined anchoring system. As far as I can tell, you organize words to trigger experiences and you use words in the same way that you would use tactile anchors. These words serve as a map for our internal maps, which are maps of the territory around you. So you are three places removed from the territory, the reality.

Now, John and Richard were always more interested in form, in the patterns of language, than in the content. They noticed that as people map their experience they have to leave certain things out. In other words, you are never going to get a truly explicit map.

There is a story about the cartography department of a small European village. The cartography department, the mapping department, was their biggest civic pride and they spent a lot of time on their maps. They decided that they would make a map that was perfect. They started making this map, and as they did it, they had to gather extensive amounts of information. The next thing they knew, they had to make the building bigger to store it all. But they kept refining their map, making it more and more detailed and pretty soon they just had to break down the walls of this building, laying out their maps all over the place. Of course, what finally happened was that the map got so big, it covered the territory completely.

The thing is, you don't need a map that big. As a matter of fact, it is okay to delete things. If you just want to find some street, it is okay to just use a street map that deletes information like hills, and deletes what kind of trees and what kind of foliage is around.

However, if you are concerned about areas to plant, and what kind of soil is around, you will want to look for a different kind of map.

People that use only visual predicates are doing this kind of thing that we are talking about with their representational systems. They are using a predicate that describes one portion of the territory—the visual aspect of that territory. Other people describe just the kinesthetic aspects, other people the auditory, and so on.

The major pattern that I am leading up to is what we call *deletion*.

A. Deletion

Deletion: that is just leaving something out. As I said, you can't make a map without leaving something out unless you want to make yourself ridiculous. You can't possibly describe in detail all of your experiences. So you start leaving things out. The only problem with that is that sometimes you delete information that is important. You have to find the right information for the right map. Most of you have heard language patterns such as, "I'm scared . . . ," "I'm confused . . . ," or "I'm bewildered," or "I'm happy." And each of those patterns deletes certain portions of what you are describing. In some cases it is to your advantage to be able to recover some of that information. Those words, "happy," "confused," "bewildered," and "scared," are in a class of words called *predicates*. They are action words—they describe relationships between things. A word like "scared" is a two place predicate. What I mean by "place" is that it is describing an action between two things. So, someone is scared of something, and that has been deleted in the utterance, "I'm scared." So, of course, if you want to recover that information, your response would be, "Scared of what, specifically?" "What is it that scares you?" Or similarly, if a person says, "I'm confused," he has to be confused about something.

In a sentence such as, "John ordered coffee and Mary ordered peas," it is okay to delete some information. Sometimes it is redundant. You don't need to say "ordered" twice, although you do have to be careful of the ambiguity in that particular phrase. If John ordered coffee and Mary peas . . . (laughter). What I am trying to say is that it is okay to delete some information, but other times deleted information is critically important. A professional communicator needs to be able to hear deletions when they occur and have the verbal tools to recover the deleted information when necessary.

One of the things we are going to be doing is trying to identify where people delete information that is important. For instance, if someone says that they're scared, it is very important to me to know what they are scared of. Or, if someone says that they are in pain, to know what is causing them that pain, and how it is causing them pain. Most of you will probably have intuitions about this. When someone deletes something, you say, "What specifically?" You will want to find out that kind of information.

1. Comparatives and Superlatives

There is another class of deletion that I want to talk about. If I were to say, "the Meta Model is the *best* way to gather information," I would be using the superlative, best, you might want to ask, "Better than what? compared to what?" If I say things like, "This is really good, this is great, this is far out, this is bad, terrible, or wrong," you will want to say, "Compared to what?" or, in response to the words for "better" and "worse," "better than what, worse than what?" This way, you get some kind of idea of how the person is making his comparisons and how much information he has gathered before making that comparison. Many comparisons are a form of deletion.

B. Unspecified Referential Index

An unspecified referential index is any non-referring noun phrase; when you delete "whom" or "what." If I say, *"They* always told me it would be *this way."* "They," who specifically? "This way," which way specifically? That statement is not specific enough. "It," and "people," are words used when you are deleting the specific person or object. Unspecified referential indicies can be collective nouns, like, "people," "Neuro-Linguistic Programming," or "geniuses."

Politicians use this kind of language all the time. If you do you can get by with saying the same things Thomas Hobbes said. He said, *"Man* is basically antagonistic." You can get away with generalizing and distorting things by using a collective noun such as "man," but if you say, "every person," and you begin to name everybody, and challenge the generalization, it isn't going to fit, because you are going to realize that this is a big generalization. I find that using these kinds of collective nouns can get pretty slippery if you are not aware of the deletion. When I first learned the *meta model* (I was studying politics at the time), the very first thing I did with it was to apply it to Plato's dialogues because of all the different ways that Socrates manipulates and uses language, deletes and distorts, and presupposes. Socrates just spins people around, because he was really good with violating and utilizing meta model patterns.

C. Nominalizations

Nominalization: Most of you have probably had some sort of experience with this word. A nominalization means that you take something that is an action, a *process,* and you *turn it into a noun*—that is a static entity or object. A typical one is something like "freedom." To say "I lost my freedom" is like saying, "I lost my wallet." You are treating freedom as if it were a thing. Similarly, saying, "the tension built in the room" is like saying, "the carpenter built in the room." You can confuse the word, tension, with something that is a thing and not the process of somebody being tense about something.

So, in a way, nominalization is a form of deletion, too, because you are deleting certain information about the process you are talking about; specifically in this case, tension or freedom. Being free to do what, specifically? Someone may say, "I am having trouble with my *life,*" or, "things are going wrong in my *life.*" Well, you can break that down. You want to turn it around and make it into a process. Living where? With whom? And, living how? You know, life is not a thing. And so, what you do with a nominalization is try and take this action or activity used as a noun or a thing and bring it back into a process. If someone says, "I am having a lot of difficulty with this relationship," you ask, "you, relating to whom?" You put it back into the verb form of "relate."

One of the ways to identify these kinds of things for yourself is to pay attention to your own internal representation of what the person says. So, if I say, "Yesterday I had an accident . . . ," does everybody understand what I am saying? Careful, I could have crashed down the stairs, I could have tripped into somebody, I could have forgotten something. I would like to get a couple of people's responses to that question. When I said, "an accident," who thought of what? What did you think of? Answer: "I cut my finger." (Robert) "Was it verbal like that?" (Answer) "No, I saw a cut finger." (Someone else) "I pictured an automobile accident." (Someone else) "Bowel movement . . . (laughter)."

Essentially, what I am saying is that, here, I used a phrase that everybody made sense of. You could understand that verbalization, but you each had different representations. As I've always said, "A word is worth a thousand pictures."

One of the things that always has amazed me is that people in therapeutic contexts, and people in business contexts, very often don't realize that. In other words, you listen to somebody say they had an accident, or "I am really troubled," and you make sense of that for yourself without really knowing the other person's representation for it.

Some people are very prone to nominalizations. Many people have what we call *blind spots* to meta model patterns. I was once in a workshop and there was a woman there who used nominalizations like crazy. She would say, "I just don't understand why my experiences and realizations don't contribute to the actualization of my frustrations in a direction that will cause an integration of my life crisis." To make a teaching point I replied, "Because of the experiential qualities of your learnings and understandings, you begin to formulate new perceptions of childhood conceptualizations and knowledge . . ." and spewed out about five minutes worth of crap, and she goes, "Oh, yeah, that is what I was thinking too." She made sense out of what I said. Everyone just started laughing because I had just sat there for five minutes thinking of all the nominalizations that I could, and she made sense of it.

If somebody just keeps going on and following what another person is saying, and, internally, makes up his own map for what that other person is saying, that map has nothing to do with what the other person is talking about. There is a phenomenon called transderivational search.

1. Transderivational Search

Transderivational search means you search back through your experiences to find a reference for what I am talking about. If you had done a transderivational search when I said, "I had an accident," you would have gone back through your personal history until you had found a reference structure for accidents. You might have gone back to an automobile accident in which you participated. That word "accident" is an anchor or trigger for a bunch of representations in your personal history, your experience. In one seminar, I asked for people's representations for the word "dog" and somebody burst into tears, because the day before her dog had died. It got hit by a car. Those kinds of things can easily happen, because words are anchors. People will refer to their own experiences to make sense of someone else's.

Now, as any one of you who has worked with hypnotic patterns knows, you use the exact opposite of the meta model when you are doing a trance induction. For instance, you take the process of nominalization and use it rampantly, because you know people will follow along anyway. So, I go along and am talking about "incorporating these new learnings and understandings in a way that is the most meaningful to you in your life today." Now, that doesn't mean anything. What are learnings? Somebody learning something specifically, through understanding what? And you want to use these to influence and create 4-tuples in that person. (I've been doing this to all of you during this presentation.)

Now, again going back to the meta model treatment of language, what you want to do with a nominalization is to make sure that it goes back into the process and then you recover what has been deleted. So, *what you do with a nominalization is put it back into process.*

Q: What if a client says there are bad *vibes* at his office?
A: "Vibes" is a nominalization. How would you put that back into process? What you want to do is ask, "What vibrating about what?" What is vibrating, and what is causing it to vibrate?" So you take the nominalization and bring it back into a verb. "Vibrating how, specifically?"

Let's say I say something like, "My love for you

is growing." How could you put that back into process? "Loving, how?" Try a sentence that didn't delete who you were loving.

You say, "I can't deal with my confusion." I respond, "What are you confused about? And how is it confusing you?" You want to put "confusion" back into a verb form, which is to make it a process again. Question: "How about making it reflexive? For instance, how are you confusing yourself?" Answer: That is presupposing that they *are* making themselves confused. That would be a pretty big presupposition, but you can get a lot of information and sort of get them thinking if you say, "How do you do that to yourself?" for something that they think is coming from the outside. My personal preference is to avoid those kinds of presuppositions.

Question: How would you turn *"accident"* into a process? Answer: Try, "What happened accidentally?" Accident is actually a little bit tricky. You accidentally do something or something accidentally occurs. "Accidentally" is actually an adverb, not a verb. But in that case it is still being used as a thing, so you want to break it down. First you will want to recover the deletions by asking, "What happened accidentally?" "Did you slip accidentally?" "Did you crash accidentally?" "Did you cut your finger accidentally?" Then you can ask, "How, specifically, was it accidental?"

Now remember, nominalizations aren't all bad. Nominalizations streamline your communication. If you acted as that department of cartography that I was talking about, and made your map that explicit, it would take you a long time to get anything communicated. In fact, sometimes in asking meta model questions you are just going to gather a lot of information about stuff that isn't important. Then you've got a *meta muddle*. I could go on and on finding out about specifics of this person's early childhood experiences and how they are broken and things that I don't need to know in order to help him change, and I could challenge a lot of nominalizations and find a lot of deletions, but they are not going to help me out that much. I am going to present, later, a way to assist you in knowing when to ask questions and what kinds of questions to ask.

D. Unspecified Verbs

Unspecified verb: Now, an unspecified verb is what you get, a lot of times, when you turn your nominalization back in to the verb form. If a person told me there was a lot of tension in the room, then what I would do would be to put "tension" back into its verb form. "Who is tensing up about what?" Now, if a person just says that he is tense or, that he is feeling very tense, he is using another form of deletion. The essential thing about an unspecified verb is that you want to ask, *"how?"* So, if somebody says, "I know that you are thinking this," you ask, "Well how, specifically, do you know?" You want to find out the rest of the pieces there. If somebody says, "Well, I just went and did this." You ask, "How, specifically, did you do it?" "Did," and "know," and words like that are verbs that are typically unspecified. So, *what you want to do is to recover the adverbs.* How, when, where did you do this, and stuff like that. And recover all those missing pieces. You ask *"How, specifically?"*

Can some people give me examples of unspecified verbs? "Give, how specifically?" you may ask. What about, "I think," "I just know it." Those are unspecified verbs because how, specifically, you *think* and the way you *know* are through your senses. You either talk to yourself about it, make a picture, or get a feeling about it. So, challenging that verb is also going to help you gather information of how people are processing information and how they are thinking. Examples: Wonder, perceive, believe, feel. "Feel" is a good example. "I felt you." "I touched you." "I kissed you." "I caressed you." If I say, "I felt something," that could be referring to any number of sensations, any number of feelings. Those other words got somewhat more specific. If you touch me, I felt your touch. "Touch" is slightly more specified as to what is going on. So is "scratch" and so is "kiss." In fact, "kiss" is the most specified of all of those, in its verbal form, because as a predicate, it implies the action, someone kissing someone. It specifies two lips touching.

These first patterns I've just presented I am going to categorize in terms of what we call *information gathering*. These are the most important and basic patterns.

Now, there are other patterns, somewhat easier to observe and challenge and are in a different class, called *limits* to a person's model. These are the kinds of words that you find when people are describing limitations in their behavior or how far they can and cannot go behaviorally.

E. Model Operators

Model operators: These are your "cans" and "cant's:" I *can* do this. I *can't* do this. I *will* do this. I *won't* do this, *must* or *mustn't, necessary,* not *neces-*

sary, and these essentially can be condensed into two categories: We have *modal operators of possibility*—It would be *impossible* to change right now, or I just *can't* tell my mother, blah, blah. I *can't* tell my employees this. You are actually saying that something is or isn't *possible*. So we have things like CAN, CAN'T, POSSIBLE, IMPOSSIBLE.

Then you have what you call *modal operators of necessity.* These are "should" and "shouldn't," "have to," "must," it is *important* that I do this. It is *necessary* that I do that.

If a person says, "I *can't* do something," you want to say, "What stops you?" You will be able to get a lot of information about the kinds of things or constraints that they have. So you have, *"What stops you?"*

The response that you offer when a person uses a modal operator of necessity and says, "must," "mustn't," or "should," or "shouldn't," is, "What would happen if you did or didn't?". Sometimes a person doesn't want to do something because he is afraid some catastrophic event would occur if they would go ahead and go through with it. So, *"What would happen?"*

Now, I've been calling these response challenges, but they are not really challenges. They are responses designed to gather higher quality information. When somebody says, "Gosh, it would be really good to do this." and, "I can do this." One of the things that you want to know is, how will they know if they are going to be able to get it accomplished. So you would ask, "What would happen if you could do it?" or, "What is going to happen when you do do it?" so that you can get information about the desired state. Determine what you are going for. What is the desired state or outcome?

F. Presuppositions

Presuppositions: where you already presuppose a thing is happening. If I say, in hypnosis, "Are you going to *go into a trance now* or in five minutes from *now?*" You are presupposing that it is going to happen. The question is just when. You presuppose that the action will occur. So, I say, "What are you going to tell me next week about how much you have changed?" By putting your attention on what you are going to tell me, I am presupposing that *you are going to change.*

If I say, "Did Bill see the cat that is on this table?" What I am asking is, did Bill see it or not, and I am presupposing that there is a cat on this table. Sometimes, people will say something like, "I would really be able to be happy if only so and so would stop making my life so painful." "If only he'd stop doing this." You are already presupposing that he is. So what you want to say is, "How do you know?" How do you know that this is occurring? How do you know that this is really going to happen? So this question is going to be, *"How do you know?"*

Since you all understand so well, already, I'll just move on. If you want to make a presupposition, all you have to do is start your sentence with "since," and whatever you say after that will have to include some presupposition.

G. Cause-Effect

Cause-effect is actually a form of presupposition, because you are presupposing that something is going to cause something else. My explanation will make you all comfortable that you understand. If I say that Mary causes me a lot of pain, or trouble, or makes me feel bad, or her looking at me like that makes me feel uncomfortable, I am presupposing that there is some connection between those two. This is an example of presupposition, because it presupposes a cause and effect relationship. When you think about it, these are the ways that we essentially have of making sense of our environment. All of our experiences are modeled in terms of cause-effect—that something is going to happen and something will result. In fact, you make extensive use of this pattern in hypnosis with post-hypnotic suggestion. "When I snap my finger *you will all wake up, vibrantly aware and alert."* Something like that. The thing is that any cause-effect relationship can be valid. If I do snap my fingers and it does make you *vibrant, alive, awake, alert,* and *energetic,* then there is a cause and an effect. But one of the things that you need to do, if you hear people saying, "She causes me so much pain," and stuff like that, is to ask, "How specifically?" "How do you know *she* does this?" and, "How, specifically, does this happen?" So, you are not just challenging the connection. You want to find out how that connection is there, how it is made. So, this is another one of those "how" questions. How do you know? And *how, specifically, does X cause Y?*

H. Universal Quantifiers

Universal quantifiers: This is one that *everybody* should know. Universal quantifiers are things like "all," "every," "never," and "always," where you are talking about something that may have happened a couple of times and you are generalizing it to all cases. People *always* go away learning so much from my seminars. By the way, all of you probably have begun to realize that there are overlaps in meta model patterns. In other words, universal quantifiers can be considered a form of deletion. Cause-effect is a form of deletion, because I am deleting how the connection is made. So that, actually, a lot of these categories overlap and include another category in them. They are actually interconnected closely.

The challenge to a universal quantifier can be made through exaggeration. You can exaggerate it and say, "It's *always* happened? Or, "You've *never, never* done this?" "Can you think of one instance where she has, or hasn't?" Or something like that where you are going to try and find counterexamples: where you want to exaggerate it into absurdity. If someone says, "She has never cared for me," you say, *"Never, ever?"* "How do you know that?"

"How do you know?" is going to be one of the real important questions for gathering information, especially when you are dealing with people's models of the world, because you will want to know how they make their maps and how they gather information.

1. The Importance of Sensory Experience

By the way, when John and Richard first invented this, they didn't know about accessing cues, so please feel free to use the information that you have available through your other sensory channels. You don't have to hear words for everything. For instance, if I ask someone, "Well, how do you know that?" and they look down and left and say, "Well, I just know it," they have given you the answer. They specifically tell you with their body. So, please use the non-verbal information. These questions are just to help gather information. You don't have to get a verbal answer to get the answer to your question.

For example, if a person looks down and right and says, "I am really confused," you don't have to say, "And how do you know you are confused?" because he is showing you. If a person looks up and left and says, "I am really confused," he is showing you how he is confused. Sometimes people will just tune in to the auditory external verbal stuff and lose a lot of other really important information that is readily available to them. Just keep all of your channels open. The whole concept of secret therapy is based on this. As they think of their problems, clients are giving you enough information with their facial gestures and tonality, so that you don't need to know in words what is going on. You can anchor the 4-tuple you see and hear, and then you can either collapse the anchor or reframe parts, or you can make a label for it. Since words are just anchors, you can create an arbitrary verbal anchor for the experience. If a client says, "You know, I have this real problem," say, "We can call that problem 'blue.' Think of what it's like when you are 'bluing.' " You actually make a label for it. What is important to you is that you know the other person has the map, that he has the representation for the experience or behavior to which you are referring. So, you can *use* the process of nominalization. You can use "blue" as a nominalization for the whole experience and as a resource, because it is an anchor as long as you can see the 4-tuple in his face and other analogues. If you say, "Think of yellow," and he raises eyes up-left, takes a breath and gestures with his left hand—then when you say, "yellow," again and he does the same things, you know he's got that representation anchored to the word "yellow."

2. The Importance of Rapport

Again, you want to temper the meta model questions with rapport. The first seminar I had with John was a linguistics class of about 150 people. John taught the meta model method in an hour or two and had everybody go out and practice it. The next week, when everybody came back to class, about 50 percent of the students claimed that they had lost all their friends, alienated their parents, offended their teachers, and so on. They had become *meta meddlers!* If you go out and ask, "How specifically do you know that you love me?" in a poor tonality, your lover may not respond the way you want. You have to have finesse and sensitivity. You can't question everything. Can you?

I. Lost Performatives

Lost performatives are similar to comparatives in that they are judgments and evaluations except that they don't always involve a comparison. Lost performatives are things such as, "that's *crazy*," "it's *bad*," "you're *resistant*." There, a person is applying a *judgment,* but is *leaving out* who made the evaluation and what criteria were used to make it. What is "lost" in the lost performative are the person and criteria that "performed" the evaluation that produced the judgment. You can recover the lost performative by asking, "Who says it's crazy, bad, or resistant?" and "Crazy according to whom and what criteria?" Some other responses to judgments could be, "Crazy compared to what?" or, "How do you know it is crazy?" or, "Would you be crazy if you did that?" We call that last maneuver *switching referential index*.

J. Mind-Reading

Mind-reading is a pattern that goes along with presupposition. If I said, "I know what you are thinking," or "You don't have to get so upset," I am presupposing that the other person is upset. I am mind-reading them. If you said, "They really hate me," you would be presupposing that you know what is going on in their heads. If I say, "You don't understand what I am saying, do you?" or "You are wondering what I am going to say next," I am mind-reading. Anytime I say, "You are thinking this," "you are wondering," or "You know this," it is another one of those presuppositions. Saying, "You all know—," is what we call mind-reading, because I am presupposing that I know what is going on in your head. It's also an example of cause-effect, because you are presupposing that some cause is having an effect on somebody else. If I said that you are causing me to feel bad, then that would be an instance of cause-effect. I could mind-read and use cause-effect. I could say, "My talking slowly causes relaxation." Then, I am still using cause-effect, but I am presupposing that it has the same effect on you that it would on me. This can be good information. When somebody is mind-reading you, or mind-reading somebody else, you can probably guess that they would respond with the same reaction that they are hallucinating in the other person.

K. Complex Equivalence

Complex equivalence is essentially finding the 4-tuple a person has for a particular word or generalization. When a person says, "She is not looking at me, she is not paying attention," he is saying that to be paying attention to him you have to be looking at him. Or, "She doesn't love me. She never tells me about her feelings." For that person, love is telling the other person about feelings. Or, "She never touches me," or, "She is never on time, she doesn't love me," or, "It hurts so bad it must be love." When someone makes two experiences equivalent, for example, "Being touched means love," you can challenge him by saying, "Have you ever known you were loved even though you weren't being touched?" Challenge the connection.

Another thing that you can do is use that how-do-you-know question. To be effective with the woman who was overweight (whom I was working with) I had to find out what would constitute, in her mind, effective therapy. In other words, what is the person's complex equivalence for what I should be doing to help them? "What do I need to do? What is equivalent to your changing?" One of the first things you do in the induction of hypnosis is to ask, "How would you know if you were in a trance?" "What is your equivalence, in terms of what you would feel, hear, or see, for what a trance state is?" Do the same thing for "change." "What would you need to see, hear, or feel to make the change that you want to?" You want to find out what set of experiences is going to mean "change," is going to mean "trance," or whatever it is you are gathering information about. In some cases, you will want to challenge it, depending on how you perceive what is going on with the person, and depending upon the intervention that you want to make.

From audience: "Give some examples of *complex equivalence.*" Answer: "If you ask that question, you don't understand something." I am saying that your asking that question *means* that you don't understand something. That may be very valid (again, this is not necessarily invalid). If I say, "You are nodding your head, you must have gotten something out of my answer," I may be accurate. I am saying that your nodding your head *means* that *you do understand,* or that *you have gotten something out of it.* Another one is: If they are fidgeting, they are nervous. So that means, fidgeting means nervousness. There may be some overlap with mind-reading.

But if I am talking about change and I say, "I can challenge nominalizations, I have changed," then I am not mind-reading, but I am saying that because I can do this, that *means* I have changed.

That reminds me of a story I heard John Grinder tell. A psychology professor he had in college was lecturing about the limitations of attention. Saying, "You can only pay attention about forty-five minutes or so," and this teacher talked on non-stop for two and a half hours on how attention span was only 45 minutes (laughter). So what I was thinking was that we would give ourselves a break and give ourselves a break. Then what I would like to do is to have you all form groups of fours and do some exercises where you will learn to identify these patterns.

Now what I am going to have you do in the exercise is this: Each of you pick one of these patterns,

The Meta Model Live

generate a bunch of them, and have the other people identify which one you are doing, and how many you are doing with each other. I want you to each practice generating these as well as challenging them.

Let's take a five minute break and be back in ten minutes (laughter). Will everybody who has studied meta model before raise your hand. What I would like to do is to have you continue raising your hands until they become cataleptic (laughter). Actually, I would like to have at least one of these people in your groups. I would like to have at least one person who knows it very well. Let's go *do it!*

(After exercise): John was doing a workshop for lawyers the other day, and my father, who is a patent attorney, was pointing out that there is a trick that a lot of lawyers do called "double questions." I say to the person on the box, "Well, you did 'x' and then you went to their house, didn't you?" The person may very well have gone to their house but I am tacking *and you did "X"* on the same question. Then the lawyer says, "Just answer yes or no," or, "Just answer the question now." If the person says, "No, I didn't," he acts like that person is being incongruent or lying, because there was this incongruent representation. Part of the statement was accurate. That is a very interesting sort of pattern. I don't think normal people use it that much.

III. Comments on the Use of the Meta Model

What I want to do is find out if anyone found out anything interesting. I would like to point out a couple of things: (1) I would like to explain the difference between mind-reading and lost performatives. When a person says, "You are tired," he is mind-reading.

"You are tired," means that I am reading into them an internal state. A lost performative is something that is a judgment. If I say, "You are bad," "You are nasty," or "You are fraudulent and unprofessional," I am not describing an internal state, I am passing a judgment.

If I say, "You are confused," I am not making a judgment as much as I am trying to identify your internal state. If I tell you that you are bad, then I am putting a judgment on you. If I say that you are tired, that is a state that you can go into. If I say that you are nasty then I'm evaluating you. A lot of mind-reading statements may have judgmental connotations. But lost performatives are generally a statement of a judgment as if it were a property of reality as opposed to a description of what is going on inside the other person. (2) Another thing is that words like "I am *patient*," "You are *confused*," "I feel *curious*," are adverbs, a class of predicates—you know adjectives and adverbs, like saying, "The grass is green." It is not like saying, "The grass is a chair." If it were really a nominalization it would fit into the same class. In the meta model you break down adjectives and adverbs like you would an unspecified verb. That is, "how specifically?"

(3) Sometimes modal operators of necessity can have a lot of bad anchors associated with them, for example, "I *should* do this, "I *should* do that." If you change those to modal operators of possibility, "I *can* do this, I *can* do that,"—it makes a big difference in the way the client feels, or the way that he thinks about it. Try saying to your clients, "I am wondering if you would substitute the word 'can' or 'want' for 'should' in the statement you just made?" Both

words share the same classification, that is they are both modal operators, but have different connotations.

(4)Complex equivalence patterns can be a positive thing, but they may also cause limitations. In a sense, it involves a limitation. I draw a direct equivalence. The person who is auditory listens to another by tilting his head to the side so his ear faces the person. The visual person says, "He is not paying attention, he is not looking at me." So, for the visual person, paying attention is the equivalent of looking. For that person "attention" is an unnecessarily limited set of experiences. Actually, "complex equivalence" could more aptly be renamed "simplistic equivalence."

(5)As an organizing principle: You've got to find a person's complex equivalence for a desired state. Ask, "How are you going to know that you've achieved your outcome?" "What specifically will be going on when you achieve your goal?" That is a positive use of it. That is important. The meta model doesn't imply that the patterns we've been talking about are bad. I use nominalizations a lot. John and Richard use nominalizations. Words are labels and labeling is in itself neither good, nor bad. The thing that is important is to know what responses they are eliciting.

(6)You are mind-reading when you leave out the complex equivalence you used to make the computation about the person's internal experience. Using accessing cues is a way to mind-read without leaving out that computation. You learn accessing cues to read people's minds more effectively.

(7)In regard to handling universal quantifiers:

Find a *counter-example,* "Was there a time when this did not happen?" If they say, "No one has ever liked me," you can provide them with an ongoing counter-example, "How do you know I don't like you?" Something like that. If someone says, "Everybody thinks I am crazy," you say, "I don't think you are crazy." In other words, you can also use yourself as a challenge, or set it up so that you can do that.

(8) Phenomenology is the philosophy of nominalizations.

(9) The meta model is perhaps one of the most profound ways that I know of to put somebody else into a trance. You are forcing them to go into downtime to recover all the deep structure. They have to go inside and do a transderivational search, age regress, and all those other things, to find the reference experience you are asking about. It is one of the fastest ways to put people into an altered state.

IV. Organizing Meta Model Questions

Now I want to provide you with a way to organize your meta model questions. When you ask people what stops them or what they want, they aren't always going to know. They will not always be able to provide you verbally with the answer to your questions. People can think of all kinds of specific reasons and give all kinds of reference experiences that may or may not have anything to do with the presenting problem. Often, when people come to me and give me reasons for this or that problem I notice that what really initiates that response is something outside of their awareness. For instance, if you raise your voice a certain degree, or you speed up the tempo of your voice and it triggers the unwanted response. They are not reacting to childhood experiences, as they suspect. There are lots of unconscious anchors in your ongoing experience.

For instance, this person whom I just worked with, a guy who owned a real estate company, was saying that he felt badly when he walked into his office and thought his employees were against him. Well, he had recently fired somebody, about six months previously, who had been in this office for a long time and was sort of vying for control as to who was going to be in charge. After that, my client became sure that the people in the office thought all these bad things about him. However, one of the first things I noticed when I walked into his office was this peculiar arrangement, consisting of a clock and some stars, on the wall. I said, "Who put that there?" He said the name of the woman he had fired. He felt guilty about firing her, because she had been there so long. It occurred to me that what happened was that he was thinking about those people around him and it wasn't them at all. It was that he walked into his office, and the first thing he would see was an anchor for this person about whom he felt guilty. He would assign the reaction to his employees because he was unconscious of the anchor—he would mind-read everybody else in the room. It was really an interesting thing. It really surprised him when we took it down and he didn't feel bad anymore.

A. Algorithm For Change

What I'm getting at is that the answers to meta model questions aren't always the answers you want. Knowing this, you can streamline the way that you ask questions. The algorithm for change is this: A client is in a *present state* now. He wants to get to a *desired state* and he needs *resources* or some sort of *transition* mechanism to get from the present state to the desired state, and that is all the information that you need to know. Now, to get this information in a high quality way is what the meta model is about. Get sensory grounded representations, that you can see, hear, feel, and smell: When I say, "I had an accident," ask yourself what you can really see, hear, and feel about *my* experience with that verbalization. Recognize that you don't want to go to your own personal history, if you are gathering information about an accident *I* had. You can't go to the time when you cut your finger and use that to make sense out of it. You need to be able to get high quality representation from me. One of the best ways that I know of to know when to ask meta model questions is to try to see, to hear, and to feel, what would be going on with that person. So, use your senses and take account of the quality of your internal representations about the client's description. Be aware of your own maps.

1. Therapist's Syndrome

Therapist's syndrome: A lot of therapists can take what they see or hear outside, in other people, and they have all sorts of programs they have developed to make interventions and to take a person from a present state to a desired state, but when it comes to themselves, they can't make images of themselves or hear themselves. All they have is this kinesthetic feeling and don't know where to go from there, because all of the programs and all of the strategies are initiated by external, visual, and auditory experiences. When I have therapists as clients, I'll often say, "Now, I want you to make an image of yourself or look in the mirror and ask yourself what you would do with a person who looked like that." A lot of times they respond immediately, "Oh, well I would do this." And then I go and do with them what they have just suggested. Do unto yourself what you would do to others. Have them do it with themselves. It is really a very profound sort of thing. It is really a simple pattern. Ask, "What would you do if this were somebody else?" and that initiates all the programs.

So, being aware of what you have and what you don't have in your own internal maps and models is going to be very important for knowing what meta model questions to ask. You can go ask for details all day. You can meta model everything and still not be able to use it to make interventions. In fact, one of the difficulties experienced by early meta modellers was gathering too much information. What do you do with all that information? So, present state desired state is the overlay that I want you to put on your information when you use the meta model. Essentially, everything else is going to be irrelevant other than present state and especially desired state information.

B. Establishing Desired States

Find out what their present state is to the degree that you can see, hear and, feel what is going on and get some representation of how they respond in a specific context. Once you have that, then say, "If you had a magic wand, what would you do differently? What would you see, hear, or feel?" This is also going to be giving them important information, because a lot of times people don't know what they would be doing differently.

John Grinder was at the liquor store buying some wine for dinner. There was a woman in there who, he said, had the external signs of someone who was an alcoholic. After he bought his wine she came up to him and asked him if he was going by the post office, although eventually what it came to was that she wanted a ride home. He said, "Sure, I'll give you a ride home." On the way there, while he was driving, she said, turning to him very quietly, "Why do you drink?" He says something like, "I like the taste with dinner. It clears the palate and stuff, but I really don't drink very much." But then, of course, being the magician that he is, he turns to her and he says, "But that isn't the real question you wanted to ask me, is it?" She burst into tears and said, "Yes, the real question is, 'Why do I drink'?" She went on and on. Not wanting this woman to keep crying in his car he suddenly shouts, "Is that your dog?" even though there was no dog there. And that brings her out of it, so that he can bring her into a state where he can communicate with her a little bit better. He proceeded to tell her some story about a little dog that he knew that was very lonely, but that dog wasn't all the way alone. There was a big difference between being lonely and being alone. Then he said, "But the question *why* do you drink is not really the question that you want to find the answer to either." And he said that he knew the question that she needed the answer to. About this time she turns to him and she says in awe, "Who are you, really?" But he just tells her, "I'll tell you the question, but what you will have to do is promise me that you will do exactly as I say. I am going to ask you the question and tap you on the shoulder and then you have to get up, go into the house and not do anything else until you write the answer down." She agrees and when they arrive at her house he says, "The real question is, 'what would you be doing if you weren't drinking'?" And he taps her on the shoulder and she gets out of the car and goes into the house. No sooner does he get home than she calls him up and says, "I've been beaten up. I have been institutionalized. I have been grilled and asked, 'why, why, why, ... ,' but no one has ever asked me that kind, kind question: What would I be doing if I wasn't drinking?" Then she said, "I was really in a bad way tonight, and I was contemplating suicide." John said, "I know." After a pause she says that she didn't really have an adequate answer to the question, yet. He told her to call him back when she got the answer. This was fairly recent, so I don't know what the final answer was, but the point of the story is that you don't need to know *why;* only *what she wants to be doing*. In terms of meta modeling, that will be one of the most important pieces of information that you can get. Any strategy that doesn't include a representation of a person's desired state is going to be useless, because you are not going to know when you've gotten the response that you want.

Here's a good example of what can happen. I was working with this woman who wanted to lose weight. She would get down to a certain weight and couldn't lose any more than that. She had even been a beauty queen at an earlier point in her life. She had been very thin and now she was heavy, so I asked her about her desired state, "What would it be like if you could get thin?" She said, "I would look like I did when I was in college. I would look like I did when I didn't like myself." Now, is it any wonder to you that she wasn't losing weight? She didn't like herself at the time she looked that way. Given this presupposition, she wasn't going to like herself if she lost that weight again, and that was the most important point of that session and of her being able to lose weight. She didn't want to be the way she was. After you get a piece of information like that you ask, "How will you still be able to like yourself and lose weight?" You use the objection to modify the desired state.

C. Eliciting Resources

To elicit *resources* ask questions such as, "Have you ever had it before? What have you done before? Did you ever have a situation like this? Has there ever been a situation where you were thin? Has there ever been a situation where you were able to respond quickly and not have to worry, and so on." In other words, you want to find out resources from their personal history. You can say, "What would it be like if you could do this?" You can create resources out of fantasy. We call this the "as if" frame.

A fantasy can be a resource, because memories and fantasies operate from the same neurology. To remember and to fantasize you use the same parts of your brain. When you fantasize an incident, you have to do it with 4-tuples, which is the same representational format that memory is all about. So, you can actually *create* resources. Role playing is another way to create resources behaviorally.

D. Goals of the Meta Model

The goals of this *META* META MODEL that we've been discussing are: (1) to find out what is going on now; what is the *presenting problem?* (2) to find out what would happen if he didn't have this problem; what do you want? What is the *desired outcome?* (3) to find out *what stops you* from getting this right now. This is actually part of the presenting problem, too. What's preventing you from getting what you want? (4) The next thing is to find out *what you need* to get over what is preventing you, or to get from the present state to the desired state. Finally, (5) *how would you know if you got it?* If you know the answer, you can get *feedback* to know if you are getting it or not. The desired state must be testable in *sensory experience.*

Question: How can you use fantasy when a person has limitations that are real, such as someone wanting to do something as unrealistic as joining a commune when he has a family to support? Answer: If you really think it's unrealistic, find his *intent* behind wanting it and try to find an alternative. It may be that what he really wants to do is be able to be happier, or be more comfortable, or something like that. Ask him what he would get out of going to a commune. If he says, "Well I would feel this way," ask him, "Well, how else can you feel that way, even if you don't go to the commune?" So, the question is, what is the outcome of that outcome, or *meta-outcome,* that the person wants. If I want to go to the moon in a sailboat, there would be a lot of things that could stop me. In that case you have to work with those limitations. In that case you *utilize* the information you've gathered. You try and find out a way around the limitation. Every limitation is just an opportunity to be creative. If I wanted to go to Mars I would ask, "If I was on Mars, what would it be like, and can I go there in a hypnotic trance, and what would the difference be?" You try and find the outcome of that outcome and see if there is some other way that you can satisfy that person. In other words, you may need time for yourself to feel comfortable, to feel that you've achieved a sense of accomplishment. Those are the kinds of things that they may be able to get some other way.

In answer to a question: I can't cure obesity by asking questions, but by getting the answers to questions that I can then utilize. Like the hypnotist who asked, What is it that you need in order to *go into a deep trance?* Some people have to be thrown into a chair and told, *"Go into hypnosis!"*

Application of the Meta-Model to the Socratic Method of Philosophical Inquiry

(1975)

By

Robert B. Dilts

TABLE OF CONTENTS

Part	Page
I. INTRODUCTION	3
II. THE META-MODEL	5
A. Natural Groupings of Meta-Model Violations	7
1. Information Gathering	7
a. Deletions	7
b. Unspecified Referential Index	7
c. Unspecified Verbs	8
d. Nominalizations	9
2. Setting and Identifying Limits	10
a. Universal Quantifiers	10
b. Modal Operators	10
3. Semantic Ill-Formedness	11
a. Complex Equivalence	11
b. Presuppositions	11
c. Cause-Effect	12
d. Mind-Reading	12
e. Lost Performative	12
III. SPECIFIC ANALYSIS OF A DIALOGUE	13
IV. GENERAL ANALYSIS OF THE SOCRATIC METHOD	23
V. CONCLUSION	26

Plato's Use of the Dialectic In *The Republic:* A Linguistic Analysis

I. Introduction

Plato's *dialectic,* a form of the Socratic method of discussion and reasoning through argument and dialogues, was described by him in *The Republic* as the "activity which systematically sets about the definition of the essential nature of things.... Dialectic, in fact, is the only activity whose method is to challenge its own assumptions so that it may rest firmly on first principles." Plato maintained that through the scrutinizing examination and re-examination of statements of principles and virtues, even those brought up by its own arguments, the dialectic would eventually boil the statements down to the eternal truths or 'forms' at their base. The success of the dialectic, however, relies on the depth of the examination and the extent to which the assumptions are challenged.

The term *'modelling'* applies to the way in which a person classifies, arranges and stores his experiences and perceptions in order to direct his actions. The way in which an individual organizes his own 'model' of the world he experiences determines the way in which past perception and experiences are recalled and how future ones are to be approached.

Philosophy and politics are ideal disciplines for the manifestation of formal modelling systems on personal and on collective levels; *philosophy* being the study and organization of one's own personal experiences and *politics* being the attempt to transform these patterns to a community level.

Plato's republic reflects one such model of the world and, in fact, *The Republic* provides for us among the first records of the conscious categorization and manipulation of a philosophical and political model.

Throughout history the great philosophers, politicians and speakers have admired and attempted to imitate Socrates' verbal artistry. Yet, there really has never been another individual who has been able to fully capture Socrates' powers of speech; his ability to identify the weak points in his opponents' arguments and assumptions; and his ability to formulate questions that so directly confront those assumptions and weak spots.

It seems that, despite its definition, the dialectic procedure was not as systematic as Plato claimed. Most people find themselves in awe of or confused by Socrates' abilities rather than able to apply the dialectic principles to their own interactions to get to "first principles." Most people are not able to really listen to what other people say and identify and challenge assumptions. Certainly this ability has not yet been made so formally explicit that anyone could be a Socrates in the same way that almost anyone can drive a car, use a gun or push a button that would detonate a nuclear explosion. Perhaps it is because of this lack that one finds it so hard to disagree with those that claim that our political systems and political thinking have not advanced much beyond that of Socrates' time—certainly not as much as our technological systems and our weaponry.

Perhaps if there had been more people trained in the Socratic ability to challenge assumptions in Hitler's Germany the course of history would have been very different.

In this paper I will apply a modern formal linguistic modelling system, the Meta-Model, to Plato's dialectic process as exemplified by Socrates in *The Republic*. The purpose of this procedure is twofold: (1) to attempt to create the beginnings of a map of Socrates' language patterns that is explicit enough that these patterns may be easily understood and recapitulated by any native speaker of English; and (2) to assess Socrates' (and thus Plato's) use of language, through the dialectic process, as a means of philosophical inquiry by evaluating just how systematically and completely the dialectic process does, in fact, challenge its own assumptions and how the process may be improved by making it more linguistically explicit.

The Meta-Model will first be applied to a specific passage from *The Republic* and an analysis will be made of the statements of the philosophical issues. Then a more general analysis will be made of the strengths and weaknesses of Plato's use of the dialectic through Socrates' dialogues.

II. The Meta-Model

The Meta-Model was developed by linguistic modellers John Grinder and Richard Bandler as a means of identifying and responding to problematic patterns in the speech of people in the therapeutic environment. It consists of a series of categories identifying various areas of verbal communication that are suseptible to considerable ambiguity and which may create limitations, confusion and miscommunication in a person's life. Use of the Meta-Model patterns is not confined to therapy, however, and can provide substantial insight into the structure of thought and speech when applied to any personal, philosophical or political inquiry.

The basic premise of the Meta-Model is that *the map is not the territory.* That is, that the models we make of the world around us with our brains and our language are not the world itself but representations of it. The Meta-Model maintains that our mental and verbal representations are subject to three basic problem areas: generalization, deletion and distortion. In language these processes occur during the translation of *deep structure* (the mental images, sounds and feelings that are stored in our brains) to *surface structure* (the words we choose to describe or represent our primary sensory experience).

The function of the Meta-Model is to identify problematic generalizations, deletions or distortions through the analysis of the syntax or form of the surface structure and provide an inquiry system so that more enriched representation of the deep structure may be attained.

The reader has no doubt noticed the parallel between the Meta-Model concept of challenging surface structure representations to get to the "deep structure" and Plato's idea of challenging assumptions to get to "first principles."

One of the goals of this paper is to demonstrate Socrates' systematic though intuitive challenges and usage of Meta-Model violations to control the flow of an argument.

A. Natural Groupings of Meta-Model Violations

In this section I will provide some brief definitions and examples of the primary Meta-Model violations in order to familiarize the reader with the identification procedures.

(NOTE: The Meta-Model is described and explained in full in the book *The Structure of Magic Vol. I* by Richard Bandler and John Grinder, Science & Behavior Books Inc., 1975.)

1. Information Gathering

a. DELETIONS—In many statements a person, object or relationship, that can enrich or even change the meaning of the statement, is left out or deleted from the verbal surface structure. For example, in the statement, "We need to increase our defense spending for purposes of international protection," a number of things have been deleted from the surface structure: Defense spending on what, specifically? Protection of whom, specifically, by whom, specifically? Increase our defense spending with what, specifically? What, specifically is the relationship between "defense spending" and "international protection?" Locating deletions in surface structure can often identify areas that have not been adequately defined, even in the deep structure of the individual or group who made the statement.

b. UNSPECIFIED REFERENTIAL INDEX—In many statements the referential index (the person, people or objects to which the statement refers) is left unspecified or unclear. For example, in the statement, *"Those Iranians* have no respect for life," the specific Iranians to which the statement is refering, have been left unspecified. In this type of distortion, the behavior of a few may become confused with the behavior of an entire group or culture. This has the tendency to dehumanize the group to which the statement is refering in the model of the speaker or listener. Some other examples of unspecified referential index could include statements like: *"People* are basically self-centered."; *"They* are responsible for the problems in the Middle East."; *"Capitalists* are only concerned with money."; *"The Communists* are out to take control of the world."

c. UNSPECIFIED VERBS—A specific mode of action is not always implied by the verb used in a statement. For example, the statement, "We need MX missiles to *keep peace* in Europe," fails to specify just how, specifically, the missiles will keep peace. Making sure a specific mode of action has been defined before a decision is made can be of critical importance.

(Author's Note (1983): A good example from modern politics of how the failure to identify and define unspecified verbs can create miscommunication and the repercussions that follow is that of the recent falling out between Ronald Reagan and Menachem Begin. An associate of the author's had the opportunity to speak with both Reagan and Begin after a Camp David meeting concerning the Lebanese crisis. His observation was that they were both satisfied with and congruent about the agreement they had made that

Begin would not interfere with Reagan's handling of the situation in Lebanon. Shortly thereafter, however, Begin criticized Reagan's policies in a televised press conference. When Reagan angrily accused Begin of failing to keep his agreement to "not interfere," Begin replied that he hadn't "interfered;" he had merely told the reporters what he thought. Here, the assumptions about the unspecified verb "interfere" were not challenged and the "first principles" or "deep structure" defining "interference" and "non-interference" were not reached and an unnecessary break in international rapport occured as a result.)

d. NOMINALIZATIONS—This is where an activity or ongoing condition or relationship (such as a verb or an adverb) is represented as an object or noun. Saying that, "We are fighting for *truth, justice* and *freedom*," for instance, is much more ambiguous than saying, "We are fighting for money." Money is a specific object that may be easily seen, felt and heard by any individual. "Truth," "justice" and "freedom" are actually words representing evaluations and relationships that may be experienced very differently by different individuals. Typically a nominalization is an unspecified verb that has been further distorted by being used as a noun. The typical way to deal with a nominalization is to put it back into verb form and recover the deletions. For example: "Who being truthful to whom about what, specifically, and in what way?" "Who treating whom justly under what conditions and in what way?" "Who being free to do what, specifically, with whom specifically?"

2. **Setting and Identifying Limits**

   a. UNIVERSAL QUANTIFIERS—Typically characterized by words like "all, every, never, always, only, everyone, everything, etc.," universal quantifiers overgeneralize behaviors or relationships observed in a few cases to characterize all such cases. The statement, "The Russians will *never* accept an arms limitation pact," exemplifies such a generalization. Some other examples include: "Building a strong army is the *only* way to prevent nuclear war." "The Japanese are *always* just ripping off U.S. technology." Such statements are typically challenged by finding counterexamples to the claim made by the statement.

   b. MODAL OPERATORS—Modal Operators are words like "should, shouldn't, must, can, can't, is necessary, impossible, etc.," where a statement is defining a limit by asserting a claim about what is possible, not possible, necessary or unnecessary. For example, the statement, "You *can't* communicate to the Chinese through any means but force," is a statement about a limitation that may or may not be accurate. A typical way to challenge modal operators is to ask questions like: "What stops you?" "What would happen if you could (or did)?" "What would you need in order to be able to?" Too often modal operators are simply assumed and accepted as existing limits. Some other examples include: "We *shouldn't* waste our time trying to colonize space." "We *must* maintain the honor of our nation even if we *must* die in the process."

3. Semantic Ill-Formedness

a. COMPLEX EQUIVALENCE—Perhaps more accurately defined as "simplistic equivalence," this type of violation occurs when two experiences become so closely tied together that they become equivalent in the surface structure of the speaker. For example, in the statement, "Automobile sales decreased again last month, our economy must really be a disaster," the speaker is implying that "decrease in automobile sales" = "economic disaster." Yet the two may not necessarily be equivalent. A more direct statement of a complex equivalencies would be, "Safety means hav- the force to destroy your enemies." Here the implication is that "safety" and the ability to "destroy your enemies" are equivalent. It is often important to challenge such equivalencies by asking, "How, specifically, do you know that?"

b. PRESUPPOSITIONS—presuppositions occur when an assumption must be held to be true in order to understand the surface structure. To understand the statement, "When the Russians stop trying to sabotage our peace efforts, we'll be able to negotiate," you must assume that the Russians already are, in fact, trying to sabotage peace efforts. Similarly the statement, "Since you leave us no alternative, we must fight," presupposes that no alternative, in fact, exists. As with complex equivalencies, presuppositions are often challenged by asking, "How, specifically, do you know that?"

12 *Application of the Meta-Model to the Socratic Method*

c. CAUSE-EFFECT—These are statements where a cause-and-effect relationship is either explicitly or implicitly implied between two experiences. Again, such a relationship may or may not be accurate. In the statement, "Acting swiftly and forcibly will *make* them respect us," it is not clear just how, specifically, the action will make the people respect the speaker. It may just as easily cause the opposite effect. Likewise in the statement, "If we don't stand firm on this position they will *make* fools out of us," one might ask "How, specifically, will they make us into fools?" Or if someone were to say, "The government needs nuclear weapons to *make* our country safe," one may ask, "How, specifically, will nuclear weapons MAKE us safe?"

d. MIND READING—In these statements the speaker claims to know what another individual or group feels, means or thinks. In the statement, "The Russians want to see an end to our way of life," the speaker is claiming to know the internal experience of a group of people—to "read their minds" so to speak. This may be more of an interpretation than a statement of actual fact. To say that, "Nixon acted out of fear in order to save his ego," would be a similar type of mind reading. To qualify the validity of the statement, one will typically want to ask, "How, specifically, do you know that?"

e. LOST PERFORMATIVE—Evaluative words such as "right, wrong, good, bad, just, etc.," tend to become disassociated from the actions and reasons that established their value in the first place. Such words can often become more dog-matic or ambiguous than useful. The individual begins to confuse his own representation of the world with the world itself. The response to a lost performative would by to ask "According to whom?" or "Bad according to what criteria" or "Best compared with what?"

It is evident that more than one of these categories may be applied to a specific word or group of words at the same time. One word may present several areas of ambiguity. Likewise, any particular statement will often contain more than one violation.

III. Specific Analysis of a Dialogue

Since it is the nature of the Meta-Model to call for extensive breakdown of the semantic and syntactic components of each sentence in the dialogue to be analyzed, it would be beyond the scope of this paper to apply it to too great a portion of Plato's book. Therefor, I have chosen to analyze a single conversational block, one which I feel is indicative of Plato's use of the dialectic, and extract the overall pattern from there.

The analysis is structured in two columns. In one column I will provide a direct transcription of the conversation from the book and in a second column, run next to the first, will be the commentary and analysis of the movement and direction of Plato's argument. The passage under study is Plato's thwarting of the conventional view of justice presented by Polemarcus through pages 56–62 of the Penguin Classics edition of *The Republic*.

It is important to keep in mind that the model is being applied to a translation and that some of the

The Conventional View of Justice:

Dialogue

Socrates: Well then, as heir to this argument, tell me, what is this saying of Simonides that you think tells us the *truth* about doing *right?*

Polemarcus: 'That *it* is *right* to *give every* man his *due,*' in that, I think he puts the matter fairly enough.

Analysis

Plato initiates his challenge of the conventional view of justice calling it 'right' at first. He also calls for 'the truth.' The usage of the term truth here is ambiguous in two ways: a) it is a nominalization in that Socrates is speaking of it as a thing rather than an adverb or judgement. b) Both "truth" and "right" are lost performatives in that it is not clear just whose set of conditions defines a statement to be "the truth" or "right," and what those conditions are.

The *italicized* words represent points where the sentence may be termed semantically ill-formed. 1) The noun argument 'it' has no referential index as to just *what* is right. As a result the statement (which is in the form of a complex equivalence) can be interpreted in two ways: a) that 'to give every man his due' is actually the only definition of the word 'right' or b) that the term 'right' is simply a value judgement of the action 'to give every man his due.' 2) 'Give' is an unspecified verb in that it is not clear just how 'due' is given. For example, one may be considered as 'giving' another person his due by not taking more than one's own due. 3) 'Every man' is a universal quantifier which may require some limiting cases. 4) 'Due' is a nominalization. It is not defined as to just what a man's due con-

S: It is indeed difficult to disagree with Simonides; he had the poet's wisdom and inspiration; but though you may know what he meant by what he said, I'm afraid I don't. For he clearly does not mean what we were just talking about just now, that we *should* return *anything* entrusted to us even though the person asking for it has *gone mad*. Yet what one has *entrusted* to another is *due* to one, isn't it?

sists of. It could be an action or a thing.

Socrates is refering to an example that he brought up previously that stated:

"But are we really to say that doing right consists simply and solely in truthfulness and returning anything we have borrowed? Are those not actions that can be sometimes right and sometimes wrong? For instance, if one borrowed a weapon from a friend who subsequently went out of his mind and then asked for it back, surely it would not be right to do so, or to consent to tell the strict truth to a madman."

In this example Socrates challenges Polemarcus' complex equivalence by finding a counter example to the universal quantifier "every man." He asserts that it would not be 'right' to return a weapon to a man who has gone mad. However, Socrates deletes the implied cause-effect relationship. He seems to be implying that it would not be right to return a weapon to a madman because the man might injure somebody, which is understandable, yet he then generalizes it to include 'anything' and adds that one should never tell the strict truth to a madman either.

Socrates appears to be confusing the interpretations of the original complex equivalence: a) that right *is* the act or b) that the act is right. He attacks the statement as an equivalency by saying that returning borrowed objects is sometimes right and sometimes wrong. Yet, what is given as a counter-example is actually a case of two different value judgements of "right" conflicting with each other. In other words, Socrates is shifting the referential index back and forth between the person who is doing the "right" act and the person to whom the right act is being done. The statement that "it is right to give every man his due" implies that right is being done to the man who is receiving his due. Socrates doesn't deny that the madman deserves his property back. What he is saying is that it is more right to prevent the possible injury of the borrower and of others than it is for the madman to get his weapon returned. So the 'rightness' of the return of the madman's property is not changed, it is simply overruled by a 'right' that is considered hierarchically more important. This, however, does not justify the generalization that anything we borrow from a madman should not be returned or that the weapon could not be returned to the man's family or guardian. Unless he is implying that objects needn't be returned to a man who has gone mad because he no longer could make proper use of them. But that would be the same as saying that it is not right to return a pair of shoes to one who has subsequently lost his feet.

It should also be pointed out that in this example Socrates has taken it upon himself to specify the verb "give" as meaning return of objects that were borrowed and defined the nominalization "due" to mean objects that have been borrowed. He also introduces an extremely ambiguous and problematic adverb 'mad' which generally applies to actions that deviate from what is considered the norm. Socrates makes no mention of degree or type of "mad-

Application of the Meta-Model to the Socratic Method

P: Yes.

S: Yet in *no circumstances should* one *return* it to a *madman*.
P: True.

S: So Simonides *must mean* something different from *this* when he says that it is right to give every man his due.

P: He certainly must

ness" nor are we given a way to determine how, specifically, we are to know if someone has suddenly "gone mad," though we are to conclude that the man is sane enough to be able to ask for his property back. In addition to this, one questions whether such an example under the conditions given is plausible enough to warrant being a valid argument.

Socrates combines the universal quantifier, "in no circumstances," with the modal operator, "should," to give his example more leverage. He is also using an unspecified verb, "return," (you could return the weapon disassembled so the madman wouldn't hurt anyone), and has nominalized the activity of behaving or going mad into "madman." Polemarcus fails to challenge any of these weak spots.

Socrates' statement is semantically ill-formed in three ways: 1) mind reading—by citing an example that he himself feels is inconsistent with Simonides statement, Socrates projects his own feelings onto Simonides and professes to know what Simonides thinks 2) he adds the modal operator "must" to his claim to be able to 'mind read' 3) he uses an unspecified referential index 'this' in a pivotal point of the statement. It is not clear whether Socrates is refering to the example of the madman or to the whole idea of the definition in general.

Polemarcus also mind reads Simonides thoughts and revises the surface struc-

for *his thought is* that one friend *owes* it to another to do him *good*, not *harm*.

ture of his statement to account for Socrates' deleted reference to the cause-effect relationship of the madman and the object which will cause him harm. It is not quite clear whether Polemarcus is actually attempting to rephrase the complex equivalence here or whether he is merely stating that he doesn't think Simonides meant his statement to apply if it meant some harm were to come between friends.

Note that he limits the scope of who is involved to just 'friends' (another unspecified referential index), and redefined the terms 'give' and 'due' so that 'to give every man his due' has become 'do friends good, not harm'—two new lost performatives. He has also inserted the unspecified verb "owes."

S: I see; then as between two *friends* one is not giving the other his *due* when he returns a sum of money the other has entrusted to him if the return is going to *cause harm*—is this what Simonides means?

Socrates restates Polemarcus' new complex equivalence and simultaneously tests the new definition of "due" against an example similar to the one involving the madman, taking advantage of the lost performative "harm." The new statement provides the means of getting around giving someone (though in this case only friends) their due if some harm will come of the action. Again, though, cause of the harm and type of harm has been deleted from the cause-effect statement.

The question that Socrates asks typifies one of his main argumentative devices. By constantly asking "yes or no" questions Socrates 1) stimulates the least amount of challenging thought in his opponent and 2) makes it much easier to draw his opponent into agreement with the whole of Socrates' statements than if he had asked something like "What do you think?" It tends to make the opponent concentrate more on getting an immediate short answer to the question than to ponder what was said. It forces an immediate agreement or disagreement.

Further, the question "Is this what Simonides means?" will lead Polemarcus to violate the Meta-Model in that a) it calls for Polemarcus to attribute his own thoughts to someone else (By getting Polemarcus to assert his own views on Simonides, Socrates can take advantage of Polemarcus' misconceptions and misinterpretations to discount Simonides. And b) it fails to qualify the unspecified verb 'mean'. To what extent does 'Simonides' mean what Socrates has said? Is Socrates' statement what Simonides is trying to say specifically or is it merely a limiting condition that Simonides inherently means as a qualification to his original statement?

P: Certainly.

Polemarcus agrees, but to *what* is still ambiguous.

S: Well then, *ought we* to *give* our *enemies* too whatever is *due* to them?

Here, Socrates switches referential index again. Socrates' purpose in asking this question is unclear. Is he a) incorporating Polemarcus' statement as a definite reinterpretation of Simonides' original complex equivalence and proceeding to challenge the limitations of the referential index 'freinds?' or b) merely questioning Polemarcus' statement as a condition applied to the original statement, "It is right to give every man his due?" The distinction is important for it makes a difference in the meaning of Socrates' question. For he could be asking 1) if we borrow something from a man who subsequently becomes our enemy, ought we return it? or 2) how does the change in the referential index from 'friends' to 'enemies' affect the meaning of 'due' in Polemarcus' statement that one friend owes it as a due to another to do him good not harm?

Notice that Socrates has replaced the condition 'it is right' with the modal operator 'ought.' In fact, the evaluative 'right' has been disassociated from the statement it is modifying 'to give every man his due' throughout most of the discussion; a) Socrates says that under no circumstances *'should'* we return anything to a madman b) Polemarcus maintains that one *'owes'* it as a "due" to do good to one's friends (the term "good," incidentally, is another lost performative and may or may not be associated with the statement 'to give every man his due.' It could imply doing good to one's friends as related strictly to giving them their due or it could apply as a generalization of all good acts, which would include such things as giving one more than his due and so forth, thus separating his statement completely from Simonides' definition). c) Socrates claims that one friend is simply not giving the other his 'due' if the return of property causes harm; there is no mention of right. Indeed, one wonders if Socrates were not arguing in favor of Simonides' definition with this last statement, for it could be interpreted that if the return of the weapon to the madman were to cause harm that it is no longer the madman's due anyway.

Application of the Meta-Model to the Socratic Method   21

This question is one of the crucial turning points in the argument, for after this the original concept of giving every man his due, the concept of proportional equality, is no longer confronted. The argument shifts to Socrates playing around with the nominalization 'justice' (which is suddenly substituted, without qualification, for the term 'right'). Much of the cause for this change comes from the Meta-Model violations in Socrates' question, 'ought we give our enemies too whatever is due to them?': 1) as was already pointed out, 'ought' was substituted for 'right,' implying a different level of judgement of the claim. 2) the referential index 'we' calls for a self-oriented opinion which also limits the level of judgement 3)'give' is still an extremely poorly specified verb refering to either a) returning borrowed objects or b) to do good to one's friends ('do' is even more unspecified than 'give,' as there could be limitless possibilities of 'doing' good) 4) 'our' as does 'we' appeals specifically to one's self-interest 5) 'enemies' is an ambiguous unspecified referential index, for, depending on what type of enemy it is, what one considers his 'due' may vary. One looks differently on former friends who have wronged us in some way than they would on 'barbarians' from another country that one has never even seen before. 6) the term 'due' is controversial as ever. Indeed, one might consider it his 'due' to an enemy to try to make amends.

P: Certainly, what is due to

Polemarcus' reply is extremely limiting to the argument: 1) he claims that

them; and that is, I assume, what is *appropriate* between enemies, an *injury* of some sort.

injury is what '*is* due' the enemy, implying that it is the only due. His earlier claim was that good was '*a* due' between friends, meaning that good was not the only due between them. 2) he admits that the answer is his subjective opinion by claiming it as his own assumption. 3) Polemarcus substitutes the equally ambiguous lost performative "appropriate" for "right." 4) 'injury' is a nominalization. How, specifically, the enemy is injured and what type of injury is not indicated.

S: It looks as if Simonides was talking about what is right with the poet's ambiguity. For it appears that he meant that it is *right* to give *everyone* what is *appropriate* to him, but he called this his '*due.*'

This time Socrates goes after the lost performative. Again, he equates Polemarcus' assumptions to be the same as Simonides' meaning.

Socrates makes four Meta-Model violations in this statement: 1) He projects Polemarcus' opinion on Simonides. It is not certain whether Socrates actually believes that this is the actual conclusion or whether he is merely leading Polemarcus on to make it easier to win the argument. It seems to be one of Plato's devices to lead the emphasis of the argument off of the major point and discount his opponent through some trick or minor exception rather than face the real philosophic problem. Often Plato will disregard an important concept because of some minor flaw. Apparently, because of his belief in the forms (classic nominalizations), Plato seems to be saying that if a statement is not entirely and 'eternally' correct as a universal quantifier it can not be allowed. 2) Socrates reinserts the value 'right' when none of the arguments have really been examined from that level. 3) He generalizes the two cases of the friends and enemies rela-

Application of the Meta-Model to the Socratic Method

tionships to include 'everyone.' 4) He fails to further investigate the term 'appropriate' and how it would apply in more specific cases, and substitutes it without any real challenge for 'due.'

Because of time and space considerations I will end the specific analysis here. As I pointed out earlier, the argument deviates from the concept that was originally proposed after this point. Further, I feel that, even in this short interchange, Socrates has exemplified many of his primary patterns.

IV. General Analysis of the Socratic Method

It is evident that Socrates (and Plato) had a highly developed ability to intuitively take advantage of the ambiguities of spoken language to get the upper hand in an argument. Even from the short passage analyzed here, it is easy to see that Socrates would systematically and successfully challenge his opponents' arguments by either (1) asking them questions in a way that forced them to violate the Meta-Model or (2) violating it himself and getting them to agree with his statement. Within the half a dozen verbalizations analyzed here, Socrates successfully challenged or utilized ambiguities involving complex equivalence, universal quantifiers, modal operators, cause-effect, unspecified referential index and lost performative.

One typical Socratic maneuver, common throughout *The Republic,* is to take an example or counter-example and challenge it by generalizing it. This was usually done by pairing up a modal operator and a universal quantifier (should always, ought never, must all, etc.) in front of the statement. A good example of this is when Socrates said that we *shouldn't always* return something or tell the truth in order to act rightly, since we wouldn't to a madman. (Incidently, if one were to use Socrates' own method on him in this instance, one could ask, "So Socrates, how does one treat the madman rightly? According to your definition it must mean that in order to give the madman his due we *ought always* to lie to him and steal his possessions.")

Because Socrates did operate so intuitively, however, his dialectic lacks the rigor of an explicit process. As one can tell from examining the Meta-Model analysis of the dialogue, many assumptions were still left unidentified and unchallenged. Socrates' inquiry into the stated complex equivalence about the nature of justice and right throughout *The Republic,* while effective, was not really thorough enough to achieve firm "first principles." Many of Socrates' challenges and questions were less direct and thus, in some ways, less effective than the Meta-Model challenges presented earlier. Rather than get to the deep structure behind surface structure representations, Socrates had a tendency to simply substitute one lost performative, nominalization or referential index for another and test out the new complex equivalence.

Socrates' strengths, and his emphasis, seem to lean more towards winning arguments than finding "first principles."

Despite Plato's claim that the dialectic process challenged its own assumptions, it seems that if an opponent failed to challenge Socrates' Meta-Model violations, he took advantage of the opportunity to win the argument rather than to challenge his own assumptions. Perhaps this is because many people have "blind spots" to certain types of Meta-Model violations. Socrates seemed most prone to mind reading, implied cause-effect statements, lost performatives, modal operators and nominalizations. One must keep in mind, however, that he may have been violating these patterns in order to leverage his argument.

Due to his belief in the "eternal forms," perhaps, Plato also seems to have Socrates avoid refining or breaking down universal quantifiers and modal operators. Rather he seems to keep trying to find the "right" ones—the modal operator/universal quantifier pair that cannot be challenged.

It should be noted that the inadequacies I have been identifying here are not necessarily due to a failure on the part of Socrates or Plato but may be due to the lack of an adequate model of the primary experience, or deep structure, to which the surface structure refers. Grinder and Bandler, for instance, equate deep structure with the sensory impressions one stores and generates in one's brain. They use the concept of the "4-tuple" to help them identify when a statement has been adequately defined.

The concept of the 4-tuple states that any word (surface structure) is only meaningful to the extent that it triggers sensory representations in the listener's brain (deep structure). For example, in order to understand the word "computer" you must access your internal experience in some combination of what Grinder and Bandler identify as the four (thus the 4-tuple) primary sensory classes: (1) sight (vision); (2) sounds (audition); (3) feelings (kinesthesis); or (4) smell/taste (olfaction/gustation). The more actual sensory representations one has associated with a word, the more legitimate "deep structure" that word has.

The goal of the Meta-Model is to refine verbal descriptions to get a representation that is testable in sensory experience and thus less subject to the ambiguities of spoken language.

The specifics of this process are discussed in depth in the books *The Structure of Magic, Volumes I & II* (Bandler and Grinder), *Precision* (Grinder and McMaster) and *Neuro-Linguistic Programming Volume I* (Dilts, Grinder, Bandler, et/al.).

V. Conclusion

As I mentioned at the beginning of this paper, the analysis presented here is only the beginning of a map of Socrates' (and Plato's) verbal artistry. The Meta-Model represents only one level of patterning that may be applied to the dialogues. There are a number of other ways in which the Socratic method can be modelled.

By making some of Socrates' linguistic patterns explicit I have attempted to provide insight into his unique power over language as well as point the direction toward some ways to enhance and refine the dialectic process.

Hopefully, through such analysis we may improve not only our understanding of what Socrates was able to do but also build new tools for our present day inquiries into the important philosophical and political decisions we face. I think that the special insight and rigor that the Meta-Model offers into the examination of language is becoming more and more essential as we move closer to a world economic and political system.

APPLICATIONS OF NEURO-LINGUISTIC PROGRAMMING IN EDUCATION

(1980)

BY

ROBERT B. DILTS

TABLE OF CONTENTS

Part	Page
I. BASIC INTRODUCTION TO NEURO-LINGUISTIC PROGRAMMING	3
II. IMPLICATIONS OF NLP FOR LEARNING AND EDUCATION	12
III. USE OF NEURO-LINGUISTIC PROGRAMMING TO ENGINEER A SPECIFIC LEARNING STRATEGY	16
IV. CASE EXAMPLES	26
V. OUTLINES OF NLP PROJECTS CURRENTLY BEING IMPLEMENTED ON LEARNING AND EDUCATION	32
1. NLP and the Treatment of Learning Disabilities	32
2. NLP and Accelerated Learning	34
3. NLP and Computer Assisted Learning	36
4. NLP and Institutionalized Education	37

I. BASIC INTRODUCTION TO NEURO-LINGUISTIC PROGRAMMING

The whole of NLP is based on the fundamental presupposition that the map is not the territory—that we as human beings make maps of the world around us that allow us to operate more or less effectively as we carry out our daily tasks. NLP is a model of the mapping processes that our brains use to organize our dealings with our environment. As we stated in *NLP Volume 1:*

> The name Neuro-Linguistic Programming stands for what we maintain to be the basic process used by all human beings to encode, transfer, guide, and modify behavior . . . "Neuro" (derived from the Greek "neuron" for nerve) stands for the fundamental tenet that all behavior is the result of neurological processes. "Linguistic" (derived from the Latin "lingua" for language) indicates that neural processes are represented, ordered and sequenced into models and strategies through language and communication systems. "Programming" refers to the process of organizing the components of a system (sensory representations in this case) to achieve specific outcomes.

Every person has his own unique map of the world and is thus unique in his behavior. The processes of learning, communication and the assimilation of culture, however, require that we share and transfer certain aspects of our maps—especially those which are most effective for the growth of the species. The

NLP approach to learning involves the explicit elicitation and installation of those maps which seem particularly well suited for the functions for which they were created. To carry this out, NLP provides an explicit mapping and notational system through which learning strategies may be recorded, and an explicit behavioral technology through which these exceptionally effective strategies may be installed in other individuals.

NLP is a model based on the principle of "modelling elegance"—a principle which maintains that the model with the fewest number of distinctions will be a better model than one with many complex distinctions. NLP then strives for elegance in its representation of human behavior. In the NLP model the basic building blocks of our maps are presupposed to be our sensory or representational systems. To quote from *NLP Volume 1:*

> The basic elements from which the patterns of human behavior are formed are the perceptual systems through which the members of the species operate on their environment: vision (sight), audition (hearing), kinesthesis (body sensations), and olfaction/gustation (smell/taste). The Neuro-Linguistic Programming model presupposes that all of the distinctions we as human beings are able to make concerning our environment (internal and external) and our behavior can be usefully represented in terms of these systems. These perceptual classes constitute the structural parameters of human knowledge.
> We postulate that all of our ongoing experience can usefully be coded as consisting of some combination of these sensory classes. In our previous work (see *Patterns II*) we have chosen to represent and abbreviate the expression of our ongoing sensory experience as a 4-tuple. The 4-tuple is shown visually as:

$$< A^{e,i}, V^{e,i}, K^{e,i}, O^{e,i} >$$

Applications of NLP in Education

Here, the capital letters are abbreviations for the major sensory classes or representational systems that we use to make our models of the world:

$$A = \text{Auditory/Hearing}$$
$$V = \text{Visual/Sight}$$
$$K = \text{Kinesthetic/Body Sensations}$$
$$O = \text{Olfactory/Gustatory—Smell/Taste}$$

The superscripts "e" and "i" indicate whether the representations are coming from sources external, "e," to us, as when we are looking at, listening to, feeling, smelling or tasting something that is outside of us, or whether they are internally generated, "i," as when we are remembering or imagining some image, sound, feeling, smell or taste. We can also show the 4-tuple iconically as:

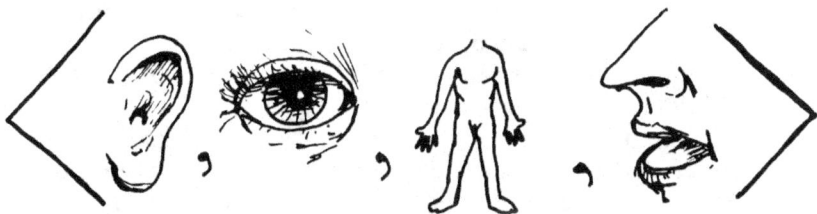

In NLP, sensory systems have much more functional significance than is attributed to them by classical models in which the senses are regarded as passive input mechanisms. The sensory information or distinctions received through each of these systems initiate and/or modulate, via neural interconnections, an individual's behavioral processes and output. Each perceptual class forms a sensory-motor complex that becomes "response-able" for certain classes of behavior. These sensory-motor complexes are called *representational systems* in NLP.

Each representational system forms a three-part network: 1) input 2) representation/processing and 3) output. The first stage, *input,* involves gathering information and getting feedback from the environment (both internal and external). *Representation/processing* includes the mapping of the environment and the establishment of behavioral strategies such as learning, decision-making, information storage, etc. *Output* is the causal transform of the representational mapping process.

"Behavior" in Neuro-Linguistic Programming refers to activity within any representational system complex at any of these stages. The acts of seeing, listening or feeling are behavior. So is "thinking," which, if broken down to its constituent parts, would include sensory-specific processes like *seeing* in the mind's eye, *listening* to internal dialogue, having *feelings* about something and so on. All output, of course, is behavior—ranging from micro-behavioral outputs such as lateral eye movements, tonal shifts in the voice and breathing rates to macro-behavioral outputs such as arguing, disease and kicking a football.

Our representational systems form the structural elements of our own behavioral models. The behavioral "vocabulary" of human beings consists of all the experiential content generated, either internally or from external sources, through the sensory channels during our lives. The maps or models that we use to guide our behavior are developed from the ordering of this experience into patterned sequences or "behavioral phrases," so to speak. The formal patterns of these sequences of representations are called *strategies* in Neuro-Linguistic Programming.

The way we sequence representations through our strategies will dictate the significance that a particular representation will have in our behavior, just as the sequencing of words in a sentence will determine the meaning of particular words. A specific representation in itself is relatively meaningless. What is important is how that representation functions in the context of a strategy in an individual's behavior.

A strategy, however, is more than just a string of representations. There are three characteristics which we have found to accompany any effective goal-oriented behavior—the individual has:

1) an explicit representation of the outcome of the strategy.

2) ongoing sensory experience so that he may assess progress toward the desired state.

3) flexibility of external behavior and internal representations so he may adapt their his to the environment.

In a strategy these characteristics are sequenced and employed in a systematic way. Representational systems are used to a) test the individual's progress toward his representation of his outcome and b) to process, compute and carry out the next step toward a desired state. These functions are best represented in the T.O.T.E. (Test-Operate-Test-Exit) model developed by Miller, Galanter and Pribram (1960). As we described in *NLP Volume I:*

> Developed by Miller, Galanter and Pribram as an extension of the "reflex arc" (the stimulus-response concept) in behaviorist theory, the TOTE model retains the basic simplicity of its predecessor but far surpasses it in usefulness as a neurological model of the formal internal processing sequence triggered by a stimulus. That is, it extends the "reflex arc" model to include a feedback operation as an intermediate activity between the stimulus and the response. As Miller, Galanter and Pribram explain:
>
> "The test represents the conditions that have to be met *before* the response will occur."
>
> If the conditions of the *test* phase (a comparison of present state and desired state) are met, the action initiated by the stimulus *exits* to the next step in the chain of behavior. If not, there is a feedback phase in which the system *operates* to change some aspect of the stimulus or of the organism's internal state in an attempt to satisfy the test once again. The test-operate feedback loop may recycle many times before the test is passed and the action exits.

The developers represented the T.O.T.E. in the following manner:

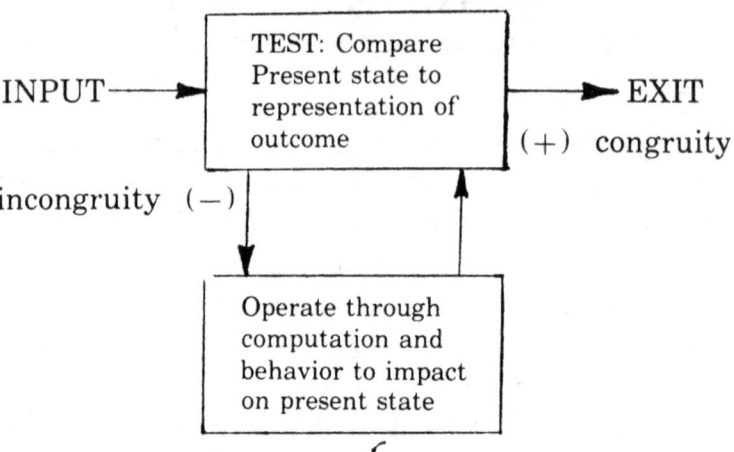

We have changed this visual representation in our own work to indicate some of the functions more clearly:

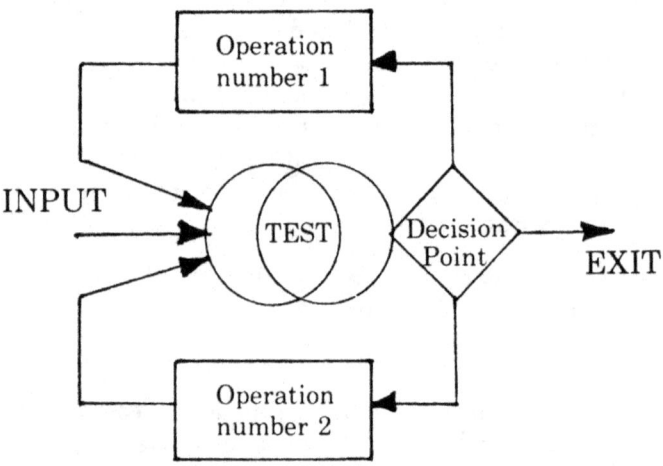

In this diagram the overlapping circles indicate a *test*—the comparison of present state to desired state. The diamond-shaped symbol indicates a *decision point* or choice point—depending on how closely the outcome has been achieved, the individual may choose one of any number of options. The rectangular boxes indicate possible *operations* —methods of computation or behavior through which the individual will again attempt to reach the desired outcome.

Our claim is that people develop programs, in this T.O.T.E. format, for all of their activities. Each of us has a strategy/T.O.T.E. for decision making, creativity, motivation, learning, reading, spelling, doing math, singing, teaching, and so on. The particular representations and representational systems that make up the specific test, operation, or decision point will determine the effectiveness of the strategy. One of the most important aspects of the NLP model is that it offers an explicit way to be able to observe and recognize strategies as they are occurring. As we single out and sequence the various representations in our strategies we manifest observable by-products in our overt behavior called "accessing cues." As we pointed out in *NLP Volume I:*

> Accessing, or tuning in to a particular representational system, is in some ways like tuning a radio. All of the various radio stations are always transmitting through their own signal frequencies, but by adjusting the internal works of our receiver, we can tune in to one signal or frequency in such a way that we pick up little or no interference from the others.
>
> *Accessing cues* are behaviors that we develop to tune our bodies and affect our neurology in such a way that we can access one representational system more strongly than the others. Just as we prepare to execute any overt behavior independently from the other choices available to us, like jumping, laughing, running or talking, by flexing our muscles and changing our breathing rates and eye scanning patterns in the specific ways that single out that behavior from all others, we operate similarly with cognitive behavior and complex internal processing. Each of us must systematically cycle through specific and recurrent behavioral cues to perform our strategies . . . There are two principal ways which we have found effective in teaching people in our training seminars to refine their ability to detect representational systems:

(1) attending to accessing cues which may be detected visually. Specifically (for the right-handed person):

accessing cue	representational system indicated	
eyes up and to the left	eidetic imagery	(V)
eyes up and to the right	constructed imagery	(V)
eyes defocused in position	imagery	(V)
eyes down and to the left	internal dialogue	(A)
telephone positions	internal dialogue	(A)
eyes left or right, same level of gaze	internal auditory	(A)
eyes down and to the right	body sensations	(K)
hand(s) touching on midline	body sensations	(K)

(2) attending to the choice of predicates selected (typically, unconsciously) by the client to describe his experience (see *Patterns, Volume I,* pages 68–76, 82–86 and *The Structure of Magic, Volume II,* part I). When describing experiences, each of us selects words to describe the portions of experience we attend most closely to. Thus, as communicators, when we train ourselves to detect which representational system is presupposed by the words selected by our clients to describe their experience, we have information which we can utilize effectively in our communication with them.

These are, of course, only two ways of learning to detect representational systems—there are many others. We have found, for example, that breathing patterns are an excellent indicator of which representational system a person is using at a point in time to organize and represent his experience to himself. During visualization, for example, the person's breathing tends to become shallow and high in the chest. Other equally useful indicators in our experience are the shifts in the tonal qualities of the person's voice, the tempo of speech, the color of the person's skin.

Figure 1 shows the basic eye movement index for a typical right-handed person.

Table 1 gives a number of examples of sensory-based predicates that may be used to identify specific strategy steps.

Applications of NLP in Education 11

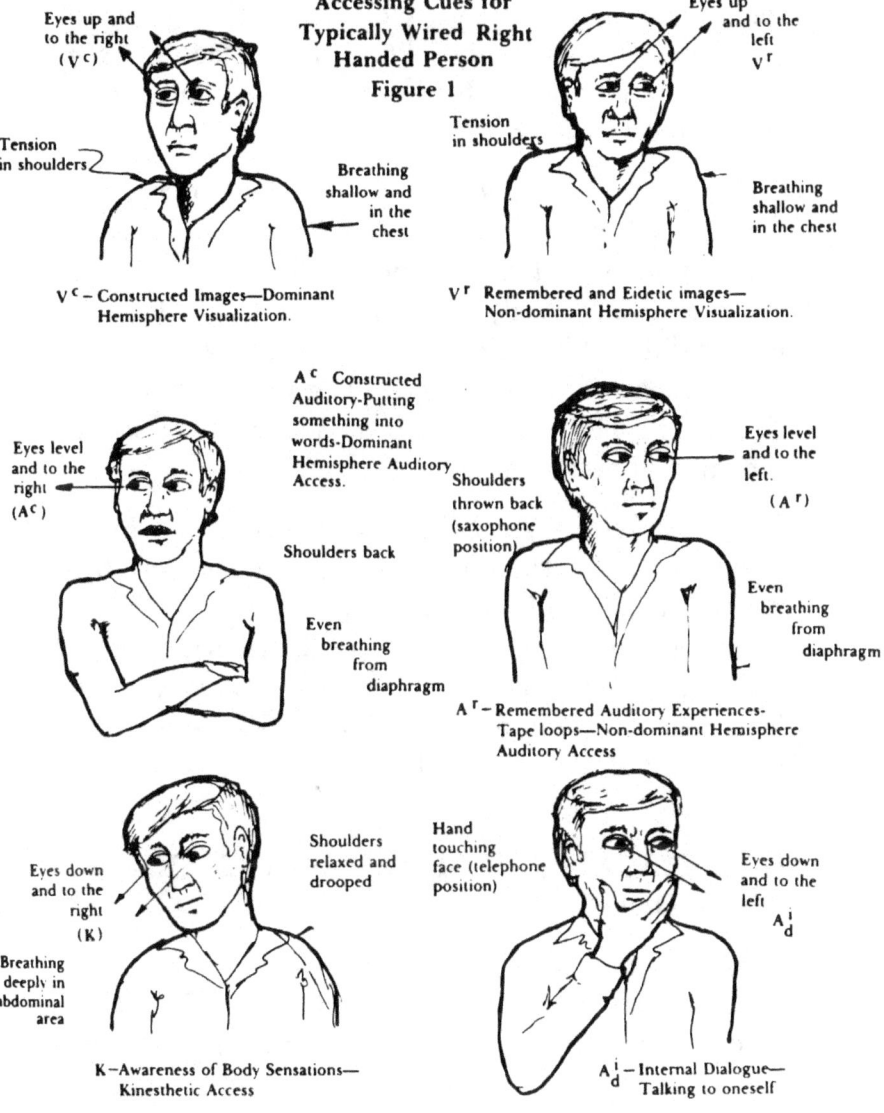

Accessing Cues for Typically Wired Right Handed Person
Figure 1

Table 1

a. *Visual*—I can *see* the pattern now; I just can't *picture* myself doing that; That *looks* like a good idea; I need a *clearer image* of the problem; I just go *blank;* That casts some *light* on the subject; *Looking* back on it now I can begin to *see* the light; An *enlightening* and *colorful* example.

b. *Auditory*—That *sounds* about right; I can *hear* your unwillingness; Does that *ring a bell;* Everything suddenly *clicked;* There's a lot of *static* inside my head; I can really *tune* in to them; *Ask* yourself if it's right and *listen* carefully for the answer; There is this idea that's been *rattling* around in my head; That has a negative *tone* to it; Something *tells* me the time is now.

c. *Kinesthetic*—I *feel* like I'm still *reaching* for an answer but I just can't seem to get a *handle* on it; It's a *heavy* problem; Things got pretty *intense;* I need to get in *touch* with my blocks; He's got a *solid* understanding of what's involved; She is so *cold* and *insensitive;* I have a *feeling* something is about to happen; *Walk* me through it.

II. IMPLICATIONS OF NLP FOR LEARNING AND EDUCATION

There is a wise saying which states that "if you give a man a fish you have fed him for the day, but if you teach a man how to fish you have fed him for the rest of his life." The job of a teacher is to install effective strategies for learning in groups of students. Until the advent of a behavioral technology as explicit as Neuro-Linguistic Programming, most of our educational process has been to teach the student what to learn but not the specific strategy for how to learn it. NLP has much to offer in terms of understanding and accelerating the learning process. First, it gives

Applications of NLP in Education

the teacher the skill with which to elicit and utilize the existing learning strategies of the students to help speed up and promote individual learning. Secondly (and in our opinion most importantly) with NLP the educational system can explicitly map out those strategies which have proven to be the most universally effective for learning the subject in question. To quote from *NLP Volume I*:

> For teachers, one important application of strategy utilization is to pace students' learning strategies in the classroom. By identifying the steps through which a student naturally incorporates new information and behavior, and by presenting the material to be taught in that form, teachers can greatly facilitate the learning process. Through adapting information to the representational systems with which a student is most adept, a teacher utilizes the student's natural skills and resources most effectively, whether at the kindergarten or college level.
>
> For example, an electrical engineer in one of our workshops, who primarily used internal kinesthetics in his strategies, described how learning to read electrical schematics was at first very difficult and boring for him. He had a hard time making sense out of the mass of lines and symbols he saw in his textbook. He couldn't "connect" with them and found circuits extremely difficult to interpret, until one day he began to imagine what it would feel like to be an electron floating through the circuit he saw diagrammed in front of him. He would imagine his various reactions and changes in behavior as he came in contact with the various components in the circuit, symbolized by visual characters on the schematic. The diagrams immediately began to make more sense to him and even became fun to figure out and to design. Each schematic presented him with a new odyssey. It was so enjoyable, in fact, that he remained with electronics and went on to become an engineer—all because he found a way to utilize his strategy effectively in the learning process.
>
> In our experience, "good" teachers use the process of pacing intuitively. Teaching is much more difficult if you have to constantly fight your students' models of the world to "reach" them.

A remarkably astute understanding of strategies was shown by a teacher in one of our workshops who had taught special education classes for several years. In her algebra class for slow and handicapped students, a large and muscular black student was having a very rough time working any of the problems on the board or on paper. (Remember that the athletic muscular—or mesomorphic—body type is indicative of a person with primarily tactile kinesthetic (K^e) strategies.) Another member of the class was blind—so all of the material presented in the class was also available in braille and raised surface diagrams. As a project, the teacher had the "slow" black student learn to read braille (K^e_d). Not so surprisingly the student's ability to pick up algebra using the braille and raised surface material was many times more rapid than when he attempted to do it visually. The braille paced his natural abilities and strategies with his tactile system (we have often suggested the use of braille and raised surfaces for sighted but kinesthetically oriented persons when we have consulted for special education groups).

Generally, kinesthetically oriented students have a difficult time in the classroom. Feelings, especially those from external sources, don't lend themselves well to what we call "academic" subject areas. One of the classic stereotypes in education is that of the athlete who has a difficult time in the visual and auditory world of lectures, blackboards and books; and likewise the thin, tense "A" student who has difficulty in the kinesthetic world of athletics. Written tests and the classroom environment are visually and auditorily oriented. In our experience many young people who have been labeled "slow," "handicapped," or "disabled" in this context are far from "stupid"—they simply have different strategies for learning that are not utilized by present techniques of education.

NLP also allows the teacher to debug existing learning strategies that are inefficient. Again, to quote *NLP Volume I:*

A good example of a representational mismatch in a strategy as the result of applying a highly valued or habitual strategy in an inappropriate context is that of a woman, with whom one of the authors was working, who had trouble with mathematics because as a child she had learned arithmetic by coding numbers kinesthetically instead of visually. Each digit from zero to nine she represented to herself as a particular feeling that matched the way she felt about herself and other people in her environment at that time. For example, "four" had the feelings of a potential prodigy that was always being suppressed for some reason; "eight" was a particularly passive number and "seven" felt very energetic to her. "Nine" was a strong feeling that matched how she felt about her mother at the time—very powerful and protective.

As she performed various arithmetic operations, these feelings would combine with one another additively or multiply to form other feelings of differing degrees of complexity and intensity. As a result, she had always found mathematics fascinating but was unable to become adept at it. For instance, she encountered difficulty in adding certain numbers together because the feelings were not compatible, and she would have to count by ones on her fingers to get the answer.

When she began to mature, her relationships and feelings changed, and her sense of particular numbers changed with them. In later years she couldn't understand why working with numbers often made her feel greatly perplexed. This strategy seriously interfered with her professional life until she began working with one of the authors to develop a new strategy for arithmetic that substituted internal visualization of the digits.

Neuro-Linguistic Programming turns the teacher from a passive presenter of information to a skilled behavioral technician.

In the next section of this paper I will demonstrate how an effective strategy may be designed and fit to a specific task.

In NLP all knowledge, thought, meaning, etc., is maintained to be the result of internal computations which consist of the overlap, correlations, and connections between representational system activity. The amount of skills, resources, and abilities we have are a direct function of the degree of development of our representational systems. One reason Einstein was able to come up with the Theory of Relativity was that he was capable of visualizing "what it would look like to be riding on the end of a light beam" (a mental task he claims that he first engaged in around the age of sixteen). A person who cannot perform a similar visual task will have a difficult time getting a representation for what relativity is all about. Could you visualize what it would look like to be passing through the room you are sitting in at the speed of light right now? As soon as there are images you cannot construct or remember or feelings you cannot construct, remember, hold, or manipulate there are tasks you cannot easily learn or perform.

By developing and expanding the full capabilities of anyone's representational systems you will evolve them as a human being. We involved in NLP firmly believe that since human beings share the same intrinsic representational capabilities it is possible to access and organize representations in order to create, achieve, or recapitulate any human phenomena. With the behavioral technology of NLP comes the very real possibility of a renaissance for the human race.

III. USE OF NEURO-LINGUISTIC PROGRAMMING TO ENGINEER A SPECIFIC LEARNING STRATEGY

We have chosen a strategy for spelling as an example to introduce the reader to the use of strategy and T.O.T.E. architecture in education. We have made this choice because spelling is a common and familiar activity that all of us engage in—the outcome of which is fairly direct and explicit.

To design a strategy the Neuro-Linguistic Programmer starts with the outcome. The outcome of spelling is to encode and output standardized sequences of visual characters. It is evident, then, that the visual representational system will play an important role in the spelling strategy.

To design a strategy to most elegantly and efficiently achieve the outcome we have identified we will need to have representations that serve as operations through which we can generate sequences of characters. We will also need representations to serve as a test to determine whether the characters we have come up with match the standard. Finally, we need a representation to tell us what to do when our test is and is not satisfied. The representations we choose for each of these functions will greatly impact the effectiveness of this strategy.

In order to choose which representational systems will serve as the most effective for the specific functions the Neuro-Linguistic Programmer will do some research. In our consulting, training programs, and personal research, for instance, we will elicit strategies from people who are consistently good spellers and from people who are poor or "disabled" spellers. By comparing this data we can then determine which representational sequences will best serve as operations, tests and decision points for the task of spelling.

Let us start by contrasting some operations for the storage and accessing of the strings of letters:

1. Sequences of letters may be stored and accessed visually. The best spellers that we have come across will almost invariably look up and left and see the whole word written or printed out. Less efficient visual spellers seem to be limited by the number of

characters they can see clearly in their mind's eye. Most people, regardless of their typical strategy, can clearly visualize—and thus easily spell—up to four or five letter single-syllable words. The number of letters a person can store visually can often be increased by having him store long words three or four characters at a time—adding the next set of four only after the previous sequence has become clearly represented.

2. Probably the most common operation used by people who are poor but not incapable spellers is that of sounding out the spelling. Individuals engaged in sounding out words will invariably orient their heads and eyes down and to the left. There are two major reasons why this type of strategy causes trouble among spellers: (a) because the operation involves breaking down the auditory pronounciation of the word each time. The speller must re-spell the word from scratch every time. This is much less efficient than simply remembering what the word looks like. (b) because of the phonetic discrepancies in the pronounciation and spelling of the English language the auditory system is not well suited for generating standardized visual sequences, as we pointed out in *NLP Volume I:*

> It has been our experience that, since the visual coding of the English language frequently does not follow phonetic rules, individuals with a visual strategy are consistently much better spellers. "Their," "there," and "they're," for example, may all be pronounced the same although visually they are different. For the phonetic speller, "ghote" may be the appropriate spelling for the word "fish"—that is, "gh" as in laugh; "o" as in women; and "ti" as in motion! The sounding out of phonics strategy may be very good for oral reading presentations where what is important is that the words are pro-

Applications of NLP in Education 19

nounced clearly; but for the specific task of spelling, it is inappropriate. The name of the system itself—"phonics"—cannot be spelled accurately with a phonetic strategy.

3. Strings of letters may be stored and reaccessed kinesthetically through the repeated writing or typing of the character sequence. The spelling then becomes coded in muscle and motor memory. This operation is actually the most efficient for *outputting* well-formed spellings. Office secretaries who type at high speeds almost never look at what they are spelling (as their eyes are on the original copy they are typing from) yet they will automatically know when they have misspelled a word because it didn't "feel right" as they were typing. The only possible setback in this operation comes when the kinesthetic speller is not allowed to write or type as they operate. (We sometimes humorously challenge kinesthetic spellers to try to spell with one hand tied behind their back.)

Once the set of characters has been generated it must be tested to find out if it is the right sequence. Again, this may be accomplished in any of the representational systems:

1. The best spellers will consistently tell you that the sequence of letters they are visualizing in their head is right because it looks the most familiar. Upon further questioning you will discover that "familiarity" is a feeling. That is, the individual will get a feeling as he looks at the image. The feeling is built as a function of how many times they have seen that spelling. Each series of letters, then, will trigger a feeling. The feeling derived from the spelling will then be compared with the kinesthetic sensation of

how familiar the spelling must feel in order to be "right." If the feeling they've gotten from looking at the word isn't strong enough they are unsure of the spelling and must operate again. An interesting difficulty arises in trying to install this test into a person who has used a phonetic strategy previously in that misspelled words are often more familiar looking than the conventional spelling.

2. Auditory spellers may often test the spelling they have come up with by sounding out the word they have just attempted to spell and comparing it with how the word is supposed to sound. Again, this is not an accurate test in that many different spellings may produce words that sound exactly alike when they are pronounced.

3. People who use a visual test in their spelling strategy will often have to write their spelling out and look at it externally (often because the image in their head isn't clear enough to look at carefully). Once the image is externalized and effort is not required to hold the image internally, a memory search may be made and the external visual representation compared with the clearest memory. People who sound out words often will actually construct a visual representation of the word in their mind (as opposed to remembering) and then compare the constructed image to memories. Such a strategy is still much less efficient than the initial direct access of visual memory.

Choice of decision point is also impactful. Naturally, decision points may also occur within any representational system:

1. People who spell well tend to have a kinesthetic decision point representation. If the spelling tests

Applications of NLP in Education

out to be correct they feel good, if not, they feel bad. In fact, they actually have a hard time reading material with misspellings because they feel so bad when they see spelling errors. Using these types of feelings as the decision point, of course, has built-in motivational properties in that if one has to feel so badly every time he sees a misspelled word he would be driven to correct it if only to preserve his own comfort while reading.

2. A person who employs an auditory representation as a decision point may say something to him like, "Oh, that word isn't spelled right." Though he may be aware of misspelled words he may not be highly motivated to correct them. Leaving words uncorrected can lead to overfamiliarity with misspellings and interfere with stored standards. The auditory decision point does not inherently lack such motivation, however. If the decision representation for a misspelled word contains a command like, "No, you better look it up," or "try again," then it can function perfectly well (and bypass the kinesthetic discomfort).

3. Visual decision point representations for spelling often consist of images as literal as seeing a big red "x" across a misspelling or a check mark next to it. Again, such a representation does not contain the inherent motivation of bad feelings.

Once this type of researching has been completed the programmer will pool all of the information together to engineer the optimal strategy design. Using the data we have presented here we can conclude that visual storage and access of the entire character sequence will be the most effective and efficient operation. Such an operation, however, is only functional if the word has been seen before. We have come across many people who will not even attempt to spell words they haven't seen. This can be limiting if an alternative operation is not also provided. We have in fact found that good spellers typically have a phonetic strategy as a backup operation if their visual operation fails. So, we will want to include the flexibility of two possible operations in our strategy and will program the choice of which to use in our decision point.

As we design our strategy we must also constantly keep in mind that our eventual outcome is to be able to install it as a T.O.T.E. in a group of people simultaneously. For instance, we may find it somewhat difficult to get a group of children to test their spelling by getting a feeling from their internal picture and comparing it with the feeling of familiarity. Also, since feelings are completely internal to the student it might be difficult for the teacher to determine whether each child is having the appropriate feeling. Another consideration is that other ongoing feelings in the person employing a kinesthetic test may interfere with the effectiveness of the operation.

It is for these reasons that we usually opt for a visual testing mechanism when designing classroom spelling strategies. Making the test visual can also make the strategy more elegant. By always putting the correct spelling in a specific place on the blackboard and using a specific color, the necessary elements for a high quality test may be included in the actual presentation of the word. The remembered image need only be tested for color and position on the blackboard.

In designing the decision point we must also keep these installation considerations in mind. For in-

Applications of NLP in Education

stance, if the child is made to feel bad when he misspells words, the task of spelling may become so uncomfortable to the child that he begins to want to avoid the subject altogether. Installing explicit sensory- based verbal instructions at the decision point is the option that we tend to opt for in classroom installations for spelling. For example, the teacher may lead the children through the strategy and after having them test their images give them instructions like, "If you can't see the picture of the letters clearly then repeat the word to yourself and look back up and left to see if the image gets any clearer ... if it is still not clear write the letters you can see on the paper in front of you and see if you can picture them in the right color." Thus, the student is given explicit auditory representations which lead to the appropriate next step in behavior without kinesthetic discomfort during the task of spelling. Let us now compare the structure of the strategy we have designed to what we discovered to be the typical strategy of the person who spells well. The typical effective spelling strategy went:

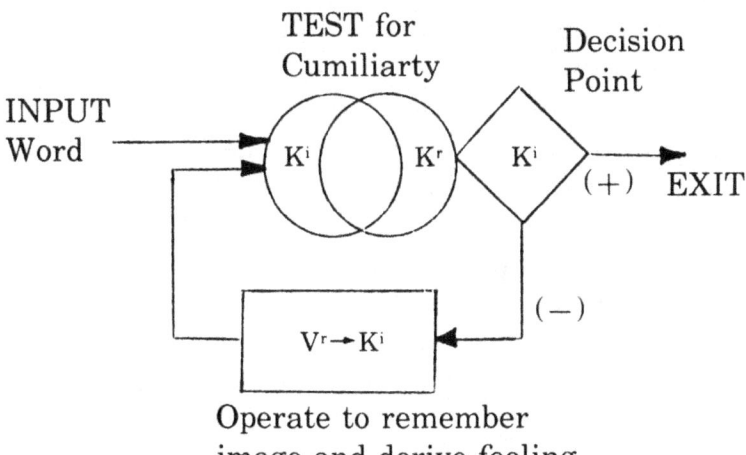

Our newly engineered strategy, on the other hand, now has the following structure:

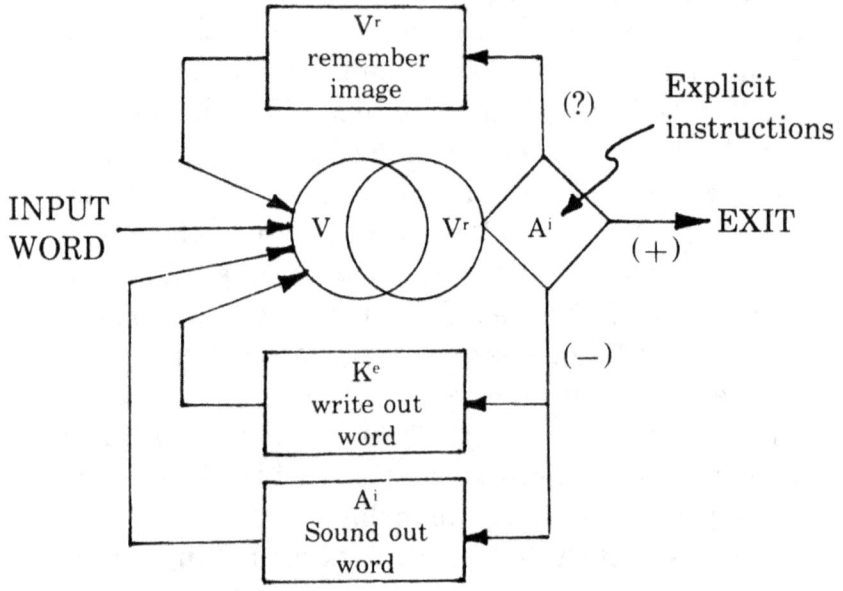

Our next step is to determine how to install the strategy in the classroom context in a group of students. Our outcome in installation is to make our strategy function as effectively and rapidly as the student's natural thought patterns. The teacher's most available tools for installation are verbal instruction and the ability to systematically direct the student's accessing cues.

We have had teachers install the strategy presented here in the following way:

1. When presenting spelling words, always use the same color to write them with and always put them in a box in the upper left hand corner of the blackboard (or write them on a large piece of paper and hang it in the upper left hand side of the wall).

2. Having the students orient their eyes up and left to look at the standard spellings, instruct them to look at each word and then close their eyes and try to see the word still in the same place, in the same color and with as much clarity as they can. Have them keep repeating this until they can close their eyes and visualize whichever series of letters they choose. The spellings have now been visually coded. As a second operation, have the students write each spelling word on a certain color paper and in a unique color. This will reinforce the visual representation and add in the kinesthetic operation.

3. Since the primary function of spelling is recognizing the standard spelling of the word, write a number of possible permutations of the spelling of the word (including the conventional spelling) in a different color and on a different place on the board. Have the students look up and to the left and discover which of the series of letters you've written on the board they can see in the upper left hand corner of the board and in the proper color.

4. If any of the students have difficulty in identifying the standard spelling, give them explicit instructions to repeat the operation of visualizing or to write them all out and find out if one feels more familiar than the others. If both of these still fail to produce the recognition, the students may be instructed to switch to the sounding out operation.

5. After you are sure the students can recognize the standard spelling, give them the words in verbal form. As you say each word have them look up and left until the image comes in the appropriate color and position. All they need to do now is to copy down

on their papers the letters they see in the picture (it's as fun as cheating!).

6. As a final step have the students switch directions and instead of copying down the letters from left to right have them spell the word backwards! This will insure that their representations of the words are actually a visual image. When you are *looking* at a word it is just as easy to read the letters off from right to left as it is from left to right. It is practically impossible, however, to sound out many words backwards (try sounding out "Albuquerque" backwards). We have discovered, in fact, that many poor spellers will initially have an easier time spelling words backwards because it reduces the interference from their sounding out strategy. Success at this step also does a great deal to boost the student's confidence and self-esteem.

IV. CASE EXAMPLES

Case Example # 1

One of the developers of the NLP spelling method had a young client once who was experiencing great difficulties in his basic scholastic skills. He was particularly poor at spelling. To check the young man's visual capabilities the youth was asked if he had ever seen the movie "Star Wars." The boy's face lit up as he exclaimed that he indeed had seen the movie. He was then asked if he could look in his mind's eye and see the Wookie, a character in the movie. The boy's eyes shifted up and left and he began describing the Wookie. He could describe everything that the Wookie did in great detail even though he had only seen

Applications of NLP in Education

the movie once! Once the boy had located his mind's eye by using the image of the Wookie he was asked to watch the Wookie open his mouth and hear the funny growling sound he made and as he did so to see the letters "W-O-O-K-I-E" printed out on the screen over his mouth. Not so surprisingly, the boy could do this easily. From then on he was directed to see all his spelling words printed over the Wookies mouth in this fashion. Whenever he wanted to spell a word, after that, he could simply look up at his "magic movie screen," and the Wookie would show him the answer. From that point on the young man consistently got high scores on his spelling tests.

Case Example #2

The following is a case example of the application of NLP to an eight-year-old child who had been labeled as having a learning disability. "Suzy" was brought to the author because she was having difficulty with reading. Suzy was being held back a grade and put into a special reading program because of her inability to read at her own grade level.

As she was first being introduced to the author Suzy stated openly that she neither liked to read nor wanted to read—that reading was difficult and other things were more fun.

The outcome of reading is to attach meaning (i.e., 4-tuples of experience) to sequences of visual characters. The visual representation of a word has no meaning independent of the associations it triggers in us. For example, "music" only has meaning for the reader in the images, sounds, feelings or smells it anchors in you. "Gefled" probably will not trigger any specific internal representations in you—except, perhaps, for confusion or curiosity. We can show this in the following way:

V^e → $<A, V, K, O>$
the written   *experience that*
word "music"   *gives the word meaning*

In having Suzy read for him it didn't take the author long to discover that she did not have internal representations attached to the words she was looking at (except for some bad feelings). Rather, Suzy's first response when viewing a word was to try to sound the word out phonetically and extract meaning from her pronounciation of what she saw. For Suzy, as for many other young students, "reading" meant to sound a word out loud in order to figure out what it meant. Often teachers confuse the ability to pronounce words with the ability to read and sight reading becomes a highly valued test of reading capability even though it may serve to slow the student down later on. We can represent this process as:

V^e → A^e → (A, V, K, O)
the written   *pronounciation*   *experience*
word   *of the word*   *that gives the*
                                          word meaning

For instance, since it was only the pronounciation that held meaning for Suzy she would continually stumble over the very same words that she had read only moments before. Rather than visually recognize them as words she had already read, Suzy could only recognize the words after she had sounded them out. Because it was such a struggle for her to sound out words that she did not "understand," reading was an unpleasant task. For Suzy, as for many people, the reading strategy that had been installed was geared toward translating a sequence of letters into a sequence of sounds rather than having the visual characters themselves trigger meaning.

Looked at from this perspective Suzy's problems were not with "reading" but rather with pronunciation. An exquisite example of this came when the author asked Suzy to read the word "fragile." After listening to her struggle with it for a short time the author told Suzy not to try to read the word any more but just to tell him what it meant, if she could. Suzy's reply was, "I think it means fragile."

Another demonstration of this came when the author had Suzy play a "word game." Suzy was to try to guess words in which letters had been left out (thus making them impossible to try to pronounce). For example, she was able to rapidly recognize "h__p__y" as "happy" even though she would struggle over the word if it was written in full form.

On the basis of the elicitation and testing of Suzy's reading strategy the author decided to install a new strategy that would make sounding out words secondary to her ability to recognize a written word and its meaning. Using flash cards, the author would show Suzy a word and turn it away much too fast for her to be able to sound it out. He would then build an experience (i.e., 4-tuple) to associate with the word. For example, when shown the word "robin" Suzy was asked to put her eyes up and to the left and visualize a picture of a bird with a red tummy hopping on a lawn pulling worms (V). Then, as she continued to watch the image, to hear the bird chirping (A). Finally, she was asked to imitate the bird in her image and hop around the room (K). As she was hopping the author would tell her the pronounciation of the word so it would become associated as another auditory portion of the 4-tuple. This process was repeated until the representation of these experiences was naturally associated with the visual stimulus of the word. Comprehension and verbal recognition were tested separately by flashing the cards and asking for either the meaning or the name of the word.

Because reading became an adventure into experience for Suzy, rather than an unrewarding attempt to sound out words, it became a fun and enjoyable part of her life. This strategy was then given to her parents and her teachers who continued the installation process. Naturally Suzy's reading improved greatly and she is currently well on her way to catching up to her grade level.

The installation of a strategy such as this does not eliminate the need or usefulness of a sounding out strategy, of course. It merely makes such a strategy secondary to recognition which is more efficient. In the event that the student does not recognize the written word what remains is the option to sound it out. In fact, an interesting by-product of the meaning-before-pronounciation strategy is that it often helps with sounding out in that knowing the meaning will automatically limit the number of possible words that the written symbols could represent and the child is able to make much better guesses at the pronounciation.

Case Example #3

Another interesting example of the use of NLP in the classroom setting involves a demonstration of the profound effects of accessing cues. A teacher came to the author about a math student who was doing quite poorly on his tests. Whenever the teacher called the student to the board to go over the problems with him, however, the student would be able to do the math without error. So that even though the student was failing his tests the teacher felt as though the student really knew the material.

Upon talking with the teacher and observing the student for a short while the author was able to easily resolve this mysterious discrepancy. When the student was at his desk taking a test he would huddle over his papers, his eyes constantly either down left or down right in auditory or kinesthetic access. When he came to the board the student would consistently write out the problem above eye level—thus forcing a visual access (which tends to be much more appropriate for processing mathematical computations).

The failing test scores were eliminated when the author instructed the teacher to have the student first practice taking quizzes by placing the test paper on the blackboard above eye level. When his abilities to compute math problems had generalized from the stimuli of chalk and slate to pencil and paper he was to return to his desk. When taking his tests he was instructed to look up and left before he answered any question and visualize himself doing the problem on the blackboard, and merely copy the answer onto his test page. Within days the young man was consistently getting perfect scores on his exams.

The impact of accessing cues should not be underestimated in classroom learning. Many a student has probably needlessly missed an answer that they should have known as the result of a teacher shouting something like, "Do you think the answer is written on the ceiling? . . . keep your eyes on the paper in front of you;" or, "don't look away while you're answering my question;" or by getting their knuckles rapped for using their fingers to process arithmetic. And there have undoubtedly been quite a few students accused of cheating while accessing auditorily.

Systematic use of accessing cues in learning could revolutionize educational procedures in the classroom setting.

V. OUTLINES OF NLP PROJECTS CURRENTLY BEING IMPLEMENTED ON LEARNING AND EDUCATION

The following are a series of outlines of learning projects currently being designed, developed, and implemented by the author and his colleagues. Such projects naturally require sufficient funding, staffing, facilities and above all interest to produce the highest quality results. If upon looking these project outlines over you would like to offer any assistance, ideas, or would like to participate in coordination with us on any of them please contact:

>NLP Research
>P.O. Box 67448
>Scotts Valley CA 95067

1. NLP AND THE TREATMENT OF LEARNING DISABILITIES

Purpose: to design and implement specific programs and strategies for the remedial and generative treatment of individuals labelled as "learning disabled."

Outcomes: a set of videotapes, a text, and a training program covering specific strategies and explicit NLP implementation and installation skills for the effective treatment of learning disabilities in the areas of basic academic performance such as reading, spelling, writing, arithmetic, mathematics and so on. (For an outline of a training program in the basic NLP skills for the installation of strategies see project #4 on NLP in institutionalized education.)

Research Method: videotaped face-to-face interviews and NLP work with individuals of varying age groups who have been labelled "dyslexic," "hyperactive," "retarded," or just "poor students" (an expansion might be made to include the blind and the deaf). During the interviews the existing learning strategies of the individuals will be elicited and examined for well-formedness. The examination will include the observation and exploration of:

(a) The degree of development of the representational capabilities of the individual—such as the relative atrophy or hypertrophy of a particular representational system.

(b) The functioning and development of the specific accessing cues employed by the individuals during the learning and performance of the basic academic skills. This will include such things as ocular-motor activity (during eye movements), ability to fixate and defocus the eyes, and other postural and motor complexes that impact on representational accessing.

(c) The specific structure of the existing strategy and T.O.T.E. sequences.

The NLP work will include the debugging of any strategies or triggers that seem harmful to the individual's learning abilities. Following this process we will discuss the installation of either predesigned effective strategies or strategies engineered and tailored to the student's internal ecology.

Follow up with respect to changes in the individual's test scores and other indicators of academic improvement will be conducted for six months to a year following the research work.

2. NLP AND ACCELERATED LEARNING

Purpose: to elicit, design, and record the most efficient and effective strategies for achieving excellence in the various subject areas of the arts and sciences.

Outcomes: a text, or "recipe book," of the most effective strategies for successful learning and performance in specific subject areas of science and art to be accompanied by a set of computer software that would help install specific strategies and representational capabilities in the user.

Research Method: interviews with a number of people who are reported masters in their chosen field will be videotaped. During the interviews and following review of the tapes the strategies of the interviewee will be elicited, recorded, and examined. These strategies will then be refined and streamlined, if necessary, for installation purposes. They will then be recorded and displayed in T.O.T.E. form along with explicit instructions for how they may be installed.

Computer software will then be designed to assist in the installation (see next project for more on computer utilization).

To date, this project has produced the following educational programs and games:

TYPING STRATEGY

Teaches you to type as quickly and accurately as a professional typist in a way that is both novel and enjoyable. Animated hands and keyboard show you which key to hit and which finger to use. Games and exercise help to increase your speed and accuracy.

LETTER MAN

Hungry Gobblers chase you around a maze at faster and faster speeds. You move by typing the letters that fill the maze. As much fun as Pac Man! Learn to type while you are playing!

BEGINNING COMPOSITION STRATEGY

Uses eye movement leads and linguistic prompts to draw out ideas and teach people about composition and creative writing in a way that is fun and easy.

COMPOSITION STRATEGY: YOUR CREATIVE BLOCKBUSTER

An advanced version of BEGINNING COMPOSITION STRATEGY. More sophisticated prompts give you more control and more options for creativity.

MATH STRATEGY

Uses the interplay between eye movement and memory to install the best strategy for memorizing basic math. Self-paced instruction helps you to learn to make lasting mental pictures.

MATH GALLERY

You direct a magic ray at mathematical formulas that move by in the colorful shooting gallery. If you hit the incorrect equation the magic ray turns it into the right one. The more you get right the faster and more challenging the game becomes.

SPELLING STRATEGY

Eye movement leads and self-paced instruction

teach you the best strategy for spelling — making mental images of the words. You'll be able to spell any word frontwards AND backwards.

SPELLING GALLERY

Shoot misspelled words in the gallery for high score and bonus points for hits in a row. A fast moving and challenging game that teaches speed recognition and speed reading skills in addition to spelling.

If you are interested in further information on prices and availability of these programs, please contact:

NLP Research
P.O. Box 67448
Scotts Valley CA 95067

3. NLP AND COMPUTER ASSISTED LEARNING

Purpose: To create computer software for microcomputers that would serve to (a) build and expand the representational capabilities of the user (b) assist in building and developing linkage and interfacing between representational systems to promote basic representational skills and (c) install prepackaged strategy and T.O.T.E. sequences in the user.

Outcomes: Computer floppy disks and tapes containing computer games and programs that will facilitate the development of representational skills and strategies in a manner that will be both systematic and fun. Different programs will be written to build the discriminative capacities of each representational system. Other programs will install synesthesia patterns and representational overlaps. Others will help to develop storage and memory capabilities of each sensory modality while others will teach the user how to construct experiences.

Another possible outcome is the development of a "Mental Health Spa" in which these programs and other machines that contribute to representational system and strategy development would be available for public use.

Research Method: Various methods, both existing and proposed, to develop the capacity of each sensory system to process stimuli with respect to detection, recognition, and comparison will be examined and evaluated for effectiveness. Methods for developing the sensory systems to detect and record patterns of repetition, variation, intensity, sequence, and timing of stimuli will also be examined and developed. On the basis of this research and NLP principles, programmed software will be designed and engineered to expand each representational system's capacity for the discrimination, duration, and amplitude of individual representations.

These programs will then be made available separately or integrated and embedded inside of programs and games designed to install strategy sequences.

4. NLP AND INSTITUTIONALIZED EDUCATION

Purpose: To create a training program to give teachers of all grade levels the NLP skills and techniques necessary for them to be able to install prepackaged learning strategies designed and engineered for the specific subjects that they teach.

Outcomes: A five-weekend training program for educators designed to give them the basic NLP skills for teaching groups of individuals. The program will include manuals for teaching (based on NLP principles) with recipes for effective learning strategies, a set of videotapes, and optional computer software.

The following is an outline of the five-weekend teacher's training program:

I. Map vs. Territory
   A. Understanding the student's model of the world
   B. Universals of the mapping process
      1. Representational systems
         a. The 4-tuple
      2. The phenomenon of consciousness
         a. 7 plus or minus 2
      3. Accessing cues
         a. Eye movements
         b. Predicates
         c. Tonality
         d. Gestures
      4. Anchoring
   C. The structure of learning
      1. T.O.T.E.s and strategies
II. Meeting the student at his model of the world
   A. Setting rapport
      1. Calibration and sensory experience
         a. Sensory-based vs. non-sensory-based experience
      2. Mirroring and pacing
      3. Matching and translating
   B. Verbal communication skills
      1. Meta-model
   C. Non-verbal communication
      1. Flexibility of analogue

III. Installation skills
   A. Design of strategies
      1. Well-formedness conditions
   B. Elicitation and debugging
   C. Platform skills
      1. Calibration—sensory experience
      2. Requisite variety
      3. Covert anchoring
      4. Metaphor
IV. Installation procedures
   A. Building representational systems
   B. Installing synesthesia patterns
   C. Chaining the sequence of representational systems
   D. Rehearsing accessing cues
   E. Giving instructions
   F. Calibrating and testing the strategy
V. Handling objections and other ecological considerations
   A. Debugging
   B. Reframing

APPLICATIONS OF NEURO-LINGUISTIC PROGRAMMING TO CREATIVE WRITING

(1982)

BY

ROBERT B. DILTS

TABLE OF CONTENTS

Part	Page
I. OVERVIEW	3
II. PRINCIPLES OF THE CREATIVE WRITING STRATEGY	5
III. THE COMPOSITION STRATEGY	6
A. Beginning the Strategy	6
B. Choosing a Beginning Sentence	9
C. Building a Prompt	9
1. Beginner	10
2. Changing Connections	12
3. Choosing Connections	13
4. Changing Perspectives	13
5. Composition Strategy	18
6. Expert	20
D. Punctuation and Grammar	21
IV. BACKGROUND INFORMATION	21

I. OVERVIEW

The Neuro-Linguistic Programming creative writing strategy can help people of all ages to get around writing blocks and help make composing and writing easier and more fun.

The NLP composition method will actually install strategies for writing by using special words and cues to direct your thought processes as you are writing. The basic procedure involves putting a key word, or group of key words, at the end of your sentence that will help "prompt" you to think of what to write next.

The prompts are constructed using special parts of speech that help to provide connections between the experiences you are writing about. Different types of these key words can be used to link your thoughts together in different ways and lead them in different directions.

You will also be moving your eyes to specific places while you are thinking about what to write. This is because recent research in the field of Neuro-Linguistic Programming has shown that people move their eyes to specific positions while they are thinking.

For instance, when people are picturing something in their mind's eye, their eyes will move up and to the left or up and to the right. When people are having internal feelings they will typically move their eyes down and to the right. When people are listening or talking to themselves inside their heads they will move their eyes straight and to the left or down and to the left.

The research in NLP also demonstrates that moving your eyes to the appropriate places can actually

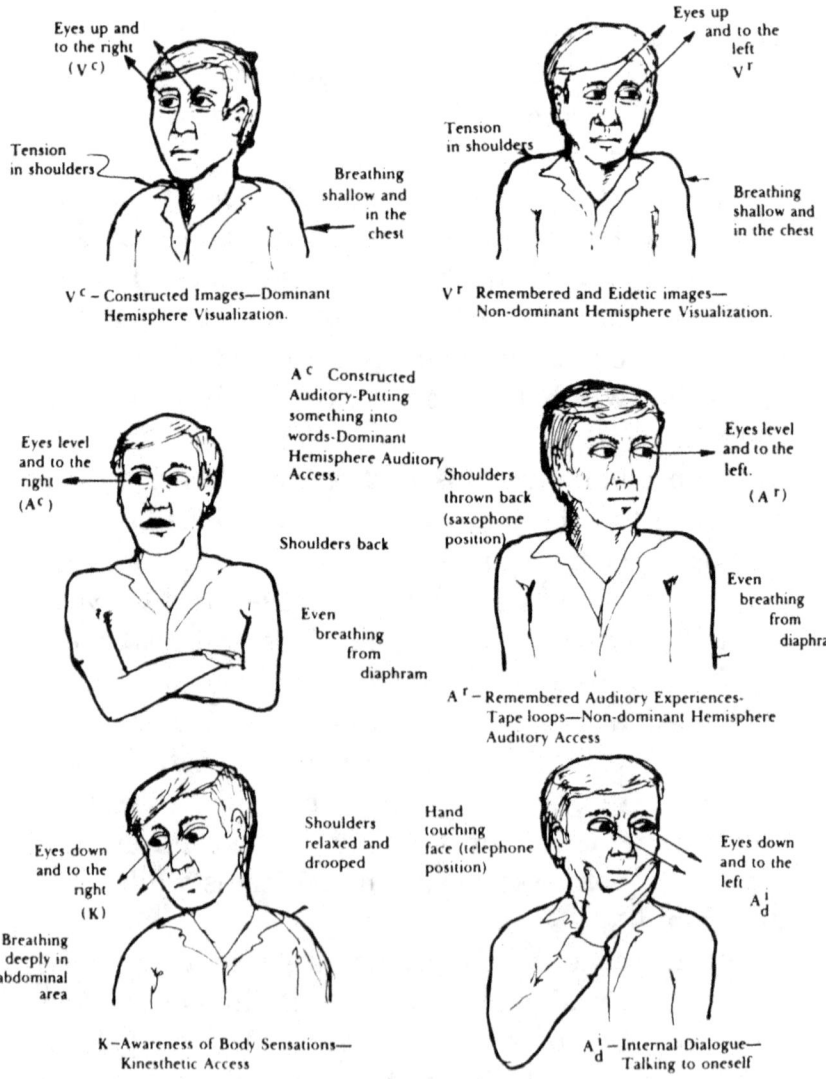

Figure 1. Accessing cues for typically wired right-handed person.

improve your abilities to think and compose more effectively.

The NLP composition strategy makes use of special words and cues to direct your thought processes as you are writing. With the strategy you make a bridge between sentences by mentally inserting a key word, or group of key words, at the end of your sentence that will help "prompt" you to think of what to write next.

The author and his colleagues have studied and mapped out the strategies of effective writers. The NLP creative writing method incorporates these strategies to help the writer organize his own mental maps as he is writing.

This particular composition strategy was intended for use by both children and adults. The insights and assistance it provides for the writing process will be valuable for both young and old writers. Some younger writers, of course, may need to be led through the program once or twice in order to get the hang of it.

Even children too young to write or type may profit from the program by having an older person read the prompts aloud. The child may respond verbally and these responses can then be recorded by the older person.

II. Principles of the Creative Writing Strategy

Good creative writing can be enhanced by the following principles:

1. FAMILIARIZE YOURSELF WITH YOUR SENSES. It is with the information gathered through our five senses that our brains create the mental maps that we use when we think. The more

you can be aware of the pictures, sounds, feelings, tastes, and smells that fill your memory and imagination, the easier it will be for you to create compositions and describe your experiences.

2. MOVING YOUR EYES TO SPECIFIC PLACES WHILE YOU ARE THINKING HELPS YOU TO TUNE IN TO A PARTICULAR SENSORY MODALITY. This is a function of how our brains work. You should learn to put your eyes in specific places as you are composing and thinking.

3. CERTAIN TYPES OF KEY WORDS DIRECT YOUR THOUGHT PROCESSES. Putting specific key words or word groups at the end of your sentence help "prompt" you to think of a next sentence. The prompts will be constructed of from one to four words, depending on the level you want to write.

5. YOU CREATE YOUR COMPOSITION BY FILLING IN THE SENTENCE YOU HAVE STARTED WITH THE PROMPT.

III. The Composition Strategy

A. Beginning the Strategy

To begin the strategy, write down the name of what you will be writing about. Once you have named the composition you will want to organize your thoughts before you actually begin writing.

First think of whether the composition will primarily be about something:

(1) YOU ARE REMEMBERING FROM THE PAST

OR

(2) YOU ARE MAKING UP

This will help to determine which direction to place your eyes later on. Memories tend to be processed in one hemisphere of the brain while constructed experiences are processed in the other hemisphere. Thus your eyes will tend to shift to the left or right depending on which type of processing you are doing (see Background Information for more details).

Next, review the experiences you want to write about in your mind a few times, focusing on a different sensory channel each time you think of the experience(s).

In addition to reviewing the experience through your different senses, think of whom you are writing the composition for and what responses you want to elicit from that person or group of people. This is an important factor to keep in mind as you are writing because it will determine many of the choices you will make about what and how to write.

Switch perceptual positions in the experience(s) you are going to write about by putting yourself behind the eyes and ears and into the bodies of different characters (first person position). What would different characters see, feel, hear, or say to themselves? Also try looking down on the characters from above (third person point of view). This is to help get you fresh ideas and different points of view with respect to the experience.

As we mentioned earlier, the creative writing strategy was modelled after the strategies of effective writers. All of the writers that we interviewed indicated that they went through a similar multi-sensory review before they started to write. The strategy of thinking about whom you are writing for was also a very critical aspect in the process of all of the effective authors interviewed. In fact, most good writers will constantly be imagining how their intended readers will be responding to what is being written.

We recommend that you do the same thing while you are writing. As you are writing, periodically imagine how your intended readers will be responding to what you have written. This will help to insure that your composition will appeal to those for whom it was intended.

After you have completed the series of preparatory exercises, determine which sensory channel was the strongest as you were thinking of your composition topic:

(1) THE PICTURE(S)

(2) THE SOUND(S)

(3) THE FEELING(S)

(4) WHAT YOU SAY TO YOURSELF

This information will, again, help to determine where to direct your eyes when you are thinking of what to write.

Using the diagram about eye movements presented earlier, determine where you will want to be putting your eyes given the sensory system you just selected above.

For example if you chose (1) THE PICTURE(S) you will be looking up. If you chose (2) THE SOUND(S) you will be looking to the side. If you chose (3) THE FEELING(S) you will be looking down and right (if you are right-handed). If you chose (4) WHAT YOU SAY TO YOURSELF you will be looking down and to the left (again, if you are right-handed).

If you ever have trouble thinking of an idea later

on while you are in the writing strategy, put your eyes in the position you just selected. This will help you to tune into the sensory system that is the strongest for you with regard to your topic and will help you think of what to write about.

B. Choosing a Beginning Sentence

Your beginning sentence will be very important, so think about it carefully. Given the way the prompts work, the whole paragraph will be based on what you have put in your beginning sentence.

One way to make a beginning sentence is to literally state the response you want to elicit from or convey to your reader.

If, for example, you were writing about computers, possible beginning sentences might include:

THIS COMPOSITION IS ABOUT COMPUTERS.

YOU WILL BE INTERESTED IN COMPUTERS.

I AM CURIOUS ABOUT COMPUTERS.

HE IS INTERESTED IN COMPUTERS.

SHE WILL BE EXCITED ABOUT COMPUTERS.

C. Building A Prompt

Now you are ready to begin the specific strategy of putting your thoughts down on paper by making prompts out of key words. There are a number of different ways of doing this that we have categorized in the following way:

1. BEGINNER
2. CHANGING CONNECTIONS

3. CHOOSING CONNECTIONS

4. CHANGING PERSPECTIVES

5. COMPOSITION STRATEGY

6. EXPERT

The differences between the various methods you may choose is a function of how the "prompt" is constructed and used. Some of the prompt modes, for instance, are designed to make you think about your composition topic in a certain way. Their purpose is to push your thoughts in a certain direction.

Other prompt modes, however, allow you the flexibility to choose a prompt that matches the direction in which your thoughts are already heading. Rather than force your thoughts in a particular direction, these prompt modes are designed to simply give the direction to your thoughts a "boost."

1. Beginner

In the BEGINNER mode you use a single word prompt to cue yourself. The BEGINNER mode uses a type of key word in the prompt that is known as a "CONNECTIVE." Connectives are words that imply or create connections between experiences. Below, we have listed the primary "connectives" that you can use.

BECAUSE

BEFORE

WHILE

AFTER

WHENEVER

IN THE SAME WAY THAT

There are other connectives in the English language, like UNTIL, UNLESS and EXCEPT. Can you think of other connectives?

In the BEGINNER method you need simply select one of the connective words. Now all you need to do is to mentally put the connective prompt you have chosen at the end of all the sentences you write down - until you end the paragraph. For example, if you have chosen "BECAUSE" to go at the end of your first sentence, "BECAUSE" will be used as the prompt for the rest of the sentences in the paragraph.

There are two ways that you can add in your connective at the end of your sentence:

1. Read the previous sentence you have written to yourself by saying it to yourself in your head. Then say the prompt word. This will create an incomplete sentence that you should fill in verbally with whatever comes to mind.

2. Pencil in the prompt word at the end of your sentence, or just above it (so that it can be erased later). Look at the incomplete sentence and fill it in.

For example, you may end up with a sequence that reads something like this:

> I am interested in computers. BECAUSE They can help people do things faster. BECAUSE They process information very quickly and can give you feedback while you are actually working on something. BECAUSE Computers use sophisticated electronic circuits called "chips." BECAUSE . . .

Just keep completing the sentences until it becomes difficult to think of a next sentence. This will become the end of your paragraph.

Without the prompt words the sample paragraph would read:

> I am interested in computers. They can help people do things faster. They can process information very quickly and give you feedback while you are actually working on something. Computers use sophisticated electronic circuits called "chips."

The purpose of the BEGINNER mode is to direct you and propel you to make a certain kind of connection between the thoughts you are having about your composition topic. The connections and ideas you will express if you use "BEFORE" to connect all of the sentences in your composition will be very different from those you will have if you use "WHILE."

As an experiment, pick one subject, like "The Space Shuttle," and write six paragraphs about it using a different connective for each one. Notice how each paragraph will lead in a different direction.

Remember, if you experience any difficulty thinking of something to say you can always position your eyes in the direction you selected at the beginning of the strategy to help you think.

2. Changing Connections

In CHANGING CONNECTIONS you use a single word prompt made from connectives like the BEGINNER mode. Unlike the BEGINNER mode, however, in the CHANGING CONNECTIONS mode you will cycle through a set sequence of connectives within the paragraph.

In the CHANGING CONNECTIONS mode you will be choosing connectives that will go at the end of your sentences in a specific sequence. The purpose

Applications of NLP to Creative Writing 13

of the CHANGING CONNECTIVES mode is to direct you to make connections about your topic within each paragraph you are writing.

For example:

> I am interested in computers. BECAUSE They can help people do things faster. BEFORE People waste time on rote processes that they don't need to do. WHILE The processes that people do best, like creativity, are put off. AFTER They fill up their time taking care of the details. BECAUSE . . .

Don't forget to move your eyes to the appropriate position if you get stuck.

3. Choosing Connections

CHOOSING CONNECTIONS also uses a single connective prompt. In this mode, however, you may choose which connective you want to use after each sentence of the paragraph, as opposed to always sticking with a specific sequence.

This method allows you the flexibility to make different kinds of connections for each sentence so that you are in much more control over the flow of connections that are made in the composition.

4. Changing Perspectives

In CHANGING PERSPECTIVES you add two more types of key words to the prompt.

The first type is known as "NARRATIVE POSITION." Changing narrative position changes the point of view from which you are writing the composition. This shift in perception is accomplished by cycling the following set of pronouns:

I

WE

YOU

THEY

HE

SHE

IT

The second type of key word to be added to the prompt is the "REPRESENTATIONAL SYSTEM" or sensory modality used to perceive the experience you are writing about. Representational system words include words like those listed below:

SEE

HEAR

FEEL

SAY

SHOW

LOOK

SOUND

You may also want to change the tense of the representational system word you are using to include words like:

SAW	WILL SEE
HEARD	WILL HEAR
FELT	WILL FEEL

In the CHANGING PERSPECTIVES mode you will be choosing the narrative position and perceptual mode that you want to use for the paragraph

Applications of NLP to Creative Writing

as well as the connective. The primary rule for this method is that, while you may change the connective word in each sentence, once you have chosen the narrative position and representational system words you want for the first sentence, you should keep them the same for the rest of the paragraph.

The prompt for CHANGING PERSPECTIVES, then, will be built out of three words: a connective, narrative position, and the perceptual mode. You will be choosing which narrative position word and which perceptual mode word you will be using only once at the beginning of the paragraph. The connective word, however, you should pick at random for each sentence.

At the end of each of these prompts you will also want to add the word "THAT" or the word "LIKE." The purpose of these words is to insure that you enter a complete sentence after the prompt. Remember, the prompts are to be taken out of the paragraph later on, so the sentences you write must be able to stand on their own.

For example:

> I am interested in computers. BECAUSE THEY WILL SHOW THAT People can develop their brains and learning capacity much more rapidly when they have the right tools. IN THE SAME WAY THAT THEY WILL SHOW THAT Because the information revolution is modelling the mind, as opposed to the industrial revolution which modelled muscle, people will learn a great deal about their own internal processes. AFTER THEY WILL SHOW THAT Our thought processes have a structure which may be made explicit and enhanced.

With this prompt method you will want to include the words "THEY WILL SHOW THAT" at the beginning of your sentence when you are thinking of your next idea. For instance, in our example above you will want to say to yourself, "THEY WILL SHOW THAT Our thought processes have a structure which may be made explicit and enhanced WHENEVER THEY WILL SHOW THAT . . ." in order to come up with the next sentence.

With this method you will want to position your eyes differently than you were before. Instead of going back to the eye position that you chose at the beginning of the strategy, you will want to place your eyes in the position that corresponds with the representational system you have chosen.

For instance, if you chose the representational SAW or SHOWED you will want to position your eyes up and to the left (remembered pictures) as you are thinking. If you chose WILL SEE you will want to look up and to the right (imagined future pictures).

The chart below will help you to connect the representational system word with the appropriate eye position:

eye position	REPRESENTATIONAL SYSTEM WORD(S)
up and left	SEE, SAW, SHOW, SHOWED, LOOK, LOOKED
up and right	WILL SEE, WILL SHOW, WILL LOOK
straight left	HEAR, HEARD, SOUND, SOUNDED
straight right	WILL HEAR, WILL SOUND
down left	WILL SAY, SAID, SAY
down right	FEEL, FELT, WILL FEEL

The purpose of this prompt mode is to help you develop new ways of looking at, talking about, and feeling about the experiences you are using as the topic of your composition. Many times, a writer will get stuck in looking at a particular experience from one

Applications of NLP to Creative Writing 17

point of view. One of the findings of NLP has been that many people tend to value one of their sensory modalities more than the others. Some people are more "visually" oriented; others will value their "feelings" most highly; while still others will rely on what they "hear" most highly.

In fact, you yourself may find that it is easier to write and get ideas using a particular perceptual position. For example, you might find it easier to write about what you FEEL than what other people might SEE or SAY. Then again, you might find it easier to think and write about what other people will SAY in the future than what they have FELT in the past. These kinds of differences will indicate a lot about the kind of writing abilities you have developed and even about what kind of person you are.

If you find that it is difficult for you to write using certain perceptual positions, use the CHANGING PERSPECTIVES mode to help force you to write from other points of view so you can develop more skill and flexibility in your writing style.

Also, think about it in terms of whom you are writing your composition for. Some readers will have an easier time understanding your composition if you write about FEELINGS; others will want you to "paint a picture" with your writing; others may enjoy and understand dialogue most fully.

Some literature teachers may want students to write about what THE AUTHOR FELT (you would want to choose the "HE FELT" prompt to write for this type of teacher). Another teacher may want to know what the material SHOWS US ABOUT THE FUTURE (in this case you would want to use the "WE WILL SEE" prompt).

Take some time and try various choices in this

mode and find out how they affect how you think. Again, practice with the ones that seem difficult at first so you can expand the elements of your style.

5. Composition Strategy

With COMPOSITION STRATEGY you will use a set sequence of prompts that are organized to sequence your thoughts about what you are writing within each paragraph. The prompt is structured in the same way that the CHANGING PERSPECTIVES prompts are, with the exception that the prompt words are to be cycled through the following specific sequence:

1) BECAUSE I FEEL THAT (eyes down right)
2) BECAUSE I SEE THAT (eyes up left or right)
3) BECAUSE I HEAR THAT (eyes straight right or left)

This sequence makes up a specific writing strategy. Once you have finished with prompt number (3) you would cycle back to prompt number (1). For example:

> I am interested in computers. BECAUSE I FEEL THAT They can actually interact with the people who are using them. BECAUSE I SEE THAT Computers will respond directly to actions that a user makes as opposed to books, tapes, or movies which are totally passive. BECAUSE I HEAR THAT It is important for people to be involved in what they are doing in order to learn most effectively. BECAUSE I FEEL THAT . . .

Again, you will want to include the "I FEEL THAT," "I SEE THAT," or "I HEAR THAT" at the

Applications of NLP to Creative Writing

beginning of your new prompt to help you formulate your next sentence.

Remember to put your eyes in the direction indicated when you are thinking of what to say.

The term "STRATEGY" implies thinking in a systematic way. The writing style of a particular person is determined to a large degree by the combinations of connectives, narrative position, and perceptual mode that he uses unconsciously in his own mind. By looking over the writing of different authors it is possible to determine the strategy that they used to write the material in terms of the types of prompts that we are varying in our composition strategies.

As we pointed out earlier, some writers may tend to write about what OTHER PEOPLE FEEL while others may write about what OTHER PEOPLE HAVE SAID. Additionally, writers may write in a consistent sequence of these perceptual orientations.

For example, a writer might first write about what he SEES. Then he may write about how he FEELS about what he sees. He may then compare how he feels with what OTHER PEOPLE have FELT about the same thing. Another writer may start by describing a FEELING and then create IMAGES on the basis of that feeling.

If you examine the writings of a specific author you will notice that they may follow a consistent pattern, such as the ones described above, over and over again. It is this type of consistency that will often define a particular style.

The COMPOSITION STRATEGY method leads you through a common sequence of perceptual orientations that will produce a particular style of writing in your composition. Try it out and notice how it compares with your typical style of writing.

6. Expert

In the EXPERT mode you have the full flexibility to choose whichever prompt structures you want. This allows you to write along at your own rate until you reach a stuck point. You may then generate a prompt by selecting from one or all of the prompt word categories - connectives, narrative position, or representational system.

Because of the flexibility of the EXPERT mode, it is possible to choose a prompt structure that will not force you to enter a complete sentence. For instance, you may choose to not have the "THAT" or "LIKE" at the end of your prompt structure. In cases such as this you will want to include a portion of the prompt structure that you have chosen in the sentence you are writing.

If, for example, you had created a set of sentences that read:

> I like computers BECAUSE THEY SHOW me how to do things in the most effective way.

You would include "THEY SHOW" in the sentence you are writing onto paper.

If the set of sentences read:

> Using this program will be easy AFTER YOU have practiced with it a couple of times.

The "YOU" would be included in the sentence that you put on your paper in order to make it grammatical.

The connectives should never be included in the sentences that you actually write down.

Note that you may choose not to have a connective word in your prompt structure at all but may want to start with a narrative position word.

Practice using various combinations of prompt words to see what happens.

It is this method that you will probably be using to write the final drafts of most of your compositions.

D. Punctuation and Grammar

As you will no doubt notice, the COMPOSITION STRATEGY is not designed to teach the proper use of grammar and punctuation but rather to help to organize your thinking so that you may be more creative and productive. We are assuming that anyone who is using this strategy will already know the basic rules of grammar and punctuation.

We believe that if you practice the strategies we have listed here you will find that you can soon write with more ease, creativity, and speed.

IV. Background Information: How and Why This Strategy Works

The principles used in the composition strategy are drawn from current developments and discoveries in the field of Neuro-Linguistic Programming—a discipline which combines psychology and neurophysiology into a powerful practical behavioral model for learning and communication.

Neuro-Linguistic Programming (NLP) is a model of how the brain functions and the impact that it has on our behavior. NLP has been applied with dramatic results in such diverse fields as therapy, business and education.

Neuro-Linguistic Programming stresses the fact that human beings organize their experience through their sensory representational systems: VISUAL (sight), AUDITORY (hearing), KINESTHETIC (feelings), GUSTATORY (taste) and OLFACTORY (smell). "Thinking," "remembering," "imagining," or "learning" all are a function of connecting, combining, accessing or storing sensory representations in our brains. One of the most interesting and important discoveries of NLP is the observation that as people tune into, focus on, or get in touch with a particular representational system they exhibit systematic and observable behaviors, called "ACCESSING CUES" in NLP. One such observable sensory cueing mechanism is eye movement. Observation and research show that the average right-handed person will consistently demonstrate the following pattern:

eye position	REPRESENTATIONAL SYSTEM ACCESSED
up and left	Visual remembered (Vr)
up and right	Visual constructed (Vc)
straight left	Auditory remembered (Ar)
straight right	Auditory constructed (Ac)
down left	Auditory internal dialogue (Ad)
down right	Kinesthetics (K)

(NOTE: Some people have eye movement cues that are reversed—notably, the majority of left-handed people. Their eye movement cues are the opposite of those shown above. That is, they look up and right to remember visual images (Vr), and look up left to construct visual imagery (Vc) and so on.)

Applications of NLP to Creative Writing

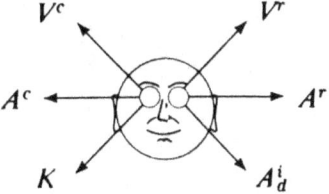

Accessing Cues

1. It is a well known (and bemoaned) fact that the people who have learned to do something most completely and effectively are typically not conscious of HOW they are doing it. In fact the degree to which one can do something without being conscious of what one is doing is most often the primary indicator of how well one has learned it. Although this phenomenon is certainly beneficial to the learner in that it frees up his conscious attention so that it may be directed on to new things to learn, it makes it difficult for the learner to tell someone else explicitly what to do. Since accessing cues are an unconscious process they may be observed although a person is not aware of what they are doing. Thus an explicit map may be charted of a person's internal processing patterns even though they themselves do not know what they are doing.

2. Because accessing cues are neurologically based they are an important tool in helping people get access to information stored in their sensory systems. The accessing position a person is in plays a critical part in helping to trigger the information they are seeking. A person who is

looking down and right (accessing feelings) and saying that he cannot SEE his way out of the mess he is in, for instance, may be assisted in doing so by having his eyes directed up and left or up and right.

By paying attention to one's accessing cues, then, our typically unconscious strategies may be modelled and taught.

Through observation of accessing cues and by explicit questioning it can be easily observed that good writers have specific strategies that they go through when they write.

These strategies may also be discovered by looking at work that an author has written and figuring out what kinds of connectives and representational systems the author would have to have been using to write what he did.

For instance, if a writer is writing dialogue, he would have to be using an auditory representational system. If a writer is describing a chain of events that he saw, he would have to be using a visual representational system, and so on.

A strategy is an explicit sequence of internal processes that occur over and over again. Once the strategy has been discovered it can be organized in such a way that a person can be led through it step by step.

The composition strategy is so explicit that it has been computerized to make it a more accessible resource. The program allows you to create, edit and print out your own stories. For information on other computerized NLP strategies for typing, spelling, basic math and basic NLP skills, contact:

NLP Research
P.O. Box 67448
Scotts Valley CA 95067

APPLICATIONS OF NLP IN HEALTH

(1983)

BY

ROBERT B. DILTS

TABLE OF CONTENTS

Part	Page
I. Introduction	3
II. Mental and Behavioral Contributors to Health	9
A. The Mechanics of "Positive Attitude"	11
1. Outcome Versus Problem Orientation	11
2. Feedback Versus Failure Orientation	14
B. Motivation Strategies	18
C. Congruence	25
1. Adaptive Intention of Behavior	26
a. Secondary Gain	30
b. Illness as Communication	31
2. Feedback	34
D. Visualization	42
1. Orientation Towards Outcomes, Communication and Congruence	42
2. Multi-Level Visualization	43
3. Using All Representational Systems	43
E. Metaphor	44
F. Epilogue	57

I. Introduction

In a recent study, cancer survivors (cancer patients who had shown no symptoms for over 10 years) were interviewed about what they had done to regain and maintain their health. The results of the interviews indicated that no one treatment method stood out as being more effective than any other. That is, some people had taken the standard medical treatment of chemotherapy and/or radiation, some had used a nutritional approach, others followed a religious path, while others used psychological methods and some did nothing at all. The one thing that did characterize the entire group, however, was that they all *believed* that the particular approach they took would work.

The relationship between mental phenomena—attitudes, beliefs, altered states of consciousness, visualization, will to live, the placebo effect, etc.—and the physical mechanics of the body have been a perplexing mystery throughout history. On the one hand, there have been innumerable examples of miraculous recoveries and unexpected, even unbelievable, physical feats that seemingly cannot be attributed to any strictly mechanical or chemical influence and must be attributed to the influence of the mind over the body. On the other hand, such examples are often highly individualized responses and are not easily repeatable or reproduceable in other people. Further, the specific steps and the exact mental processes used to attain success are often too unclear or metaphoric to be formalized into a systematic model. Medical Science has shied away from fully utilizing the placebo effect, visualization and psychological attitude largely because the responses of individual patients are too unpredictable.

The developers of Neuro-Linguistic Programming (NLP) believe that the systematic use of mental processes in promoting and maintaining health has gone untapped largely because an adequate model of how brain and bodily processes interact with one another has not yet been developed. Most psychological models present mental phenomena as being too "transcendant" and amorphous to ever be a useful physiological tool. Physical models are often too mechanistic to account for or allow for the influence of mental activity. The goal of NLP has been to try to connect our behavioral and physiological responses to the neurological (mental) processes that underly them.

The model of NLP maintains that our brains and our bodies are two interdependent and intricately interwoven parts of the same biological system. Any psychological or physical model that attempts to separate "body" and "mind" will invariably end up with a "bind." NLP offers many pragmatic skills and strategies that can help people to use their bodies and minds as an integrated whole to achieve and maintain mental and physical health.

In NLP, "thinking" is defined as the activation of our brains, a physical entity. Our "subjective experience" is made up of the systematic storage, retrieval and construction of sensory impressions in our representational systems. *"Representational System"* is an NLP term that stands for the parts of our brains responsible for processing the information transmitted through each of our five senses: sight (vision), sound (audition), feeling (kinesthesis), taste (gustation) and smell (olfaction). NLP maintains that it is the sequential accessing of specific sensory experiences in these parts of our brains that make up the mental "strategies" we use to respond to the world around us, and that these strategies constitute the most critical aspect of how our brains control our intentional and autonomic responses. As we pointed out in *NLP Vol I:*

Many studies in recent years have shown that a surprisingly high percentage of modern illnesses have stress related causes. A significant percentage of heart and circulatory problems, ulcers, arthritis, migrane headaches, eye problems and other physical symptoms have been shown to be directly related to stress, a natural outcome of many people's existing strategies. Stress can be very functional (it is not inherently "bad") as a motivator and as a test mechanism.

For us "mind" (neurological processes) and "body" (the machinery governed by these neurological processes) are an interconnected part of the same biological system. [Mental] Strategies are not merely cognitive activities within our representational systems. Our representational systems interface with other neural systems such that the neurological outcomes of our strategies affect our motor responses, respiration, autonomic control of glandular secretions, body chemistry, heart and blood pressure, metabolism and even the immune system. The neural activity in one part of our biological system cannot *not* have some effect on the rest of the system.

Neuro-Linguistic Programming is a powerful resource for preventive medicine and in the treatment of psychosomatic illness. Psychosomatic illnesses are, by definition, not "all in the mind," but are the result of real interactions between biological systems.

By changing the way people guide and organize their behavior neurologically, through their strategies, (which involves changes in accessing cues and outcomes) people reorganize themselves physiologically. In our therapeutic work we have encountered instances, time and again, in which people we have been working with have had physical symptoms improve, clear up or go into remission when they have changed an old strategy, installed a new one, or utilized a forgotten resource strategy. Symptoms have ranged from minor colds, coughs, infections and warts to arthritis, nearsightedness, tumors and cancer.

Psychological attitude has long been recognized in the medical and health professions as a contributor to the ease and speed with which someone is able to recover. With NLP we are dealing with processes more encompassing and profound than simply attitude. Using NLP we have helped people to interrupt strategies that were contributing to the ailment and to design and implement strategies used to control and regulate major aspects of their physiological ailments. We have found (not surprisingly) that people who have similar strategies are prone to similar illnesses, and that one can predict the kinds of sicknesses a person with a certain set of strategies is most likely to get.

One effective tactic is to find an individual who has been able to recover easily and rapidly from a particular illness and model his strategies (for motivation, self-feedback, etc.), then teach these strategies or install them in others with the same sickness. In our workshops we sometimes conduct an exercise in which people who have completely recovered from former chronic ailments such as allergies or poor eyesight are paired up with individuals confronted with the same problem the others used to have. The task for the person who would like to get over his allergies, headaches, nearsightedness, etc., is to elicit the steps in the strategy that his partner has used. Once this is accomplished, it is his partner's task to help him install the strategy he has just elicited. We have had many startling successes with this exercise.

We are in no way, of course, trying to discourage people from seeking proper medical assistance for physical ailments. What we are trying to communicate is that surgery, medication and other forms of chemotherapy treat physiology directly and may fail to utilize fully the potential effectiveness of self-regulation or control, or other avenues of symptom treatment. The cause for many physical symptoms can be traced to behavioral patterns and can be alleviated through alterations in behavior. The advent of biofeedback has produced abundant evidence that people can control autonomic physiological processes to a much greater degree than was believed possible a few years ago. There are many areas where culturally and institutionally accepted limitations can be successfully and usefully challenged. The primary goal of NLP is to continue the evolutionary process of challenging limitations and to move more and more parameters of our experience from environmental variables (those outside our control) to decision variables (those within our personal control). When given the choice we would always opt for the avenue of treatment emphasizing internal personal control over those involving external factors outside of our control.

Innumerable accounts of the placebo effect seem to indicate that there are classes of symptoms and pathological processes that people may be able to cure on their own, without the use of active drugs.

Certainly, much can be done behaviorally to prevent illness. The development and installation of strategies that encourage finer discriminations in, and a larger vocabulary for, proprioceptive feedback can assist in gaining more direct access to forms of self-examination and regulation . . .

The ability to discern strategies and establish rapport can be critically important for many of a physician's duties like prescribing treatments to the patient and for informed consent, where the doctor must tell the patient the risks of his or her operation or treatment. The strategies of an individual patient will determine how you should package the information to be communicated to him. Some people, if you tell them there is a greater than 50% chance of death or serious impairment, will become depressed, apathetic or fatalistic (their strategy tends to carry out the weaker part of a statistic). Such persons may incorporate the statistics as self-fulfilling. For patients who have a polarity strategy, however, it may be useful to tell them they could die, to stimulate them to flip polarities to access the resources they need to recover from or change their condition.

Some patients will suddenly adopt symptoms if

you describe them in too much detail or with too much emphasis.

If a heart patient uses stress as a motivator, he will also build up stress as a means to motivate himself to relax and exercise more! (This is the "hurry up and relax . . . or else" syndrome.)

It is important, then, for the physician to establish rapport with patients and gather information about patients' strategies before presenting them with consequential information. It is always a good idea to elicit and anchor a resource strategy with the patient. The strategy may then be reaccessed and utilized in situations that may be difficult or important.

II. Mental and Behavioral Contributors to Health

The purpose of this paper is to outline some of the strategies and principles for maintaining health that have been formalized through the application of NLP modelling principles to the area of health. While it is beyond the scope of this work to cover all of the many ways NLP has been used to promote health and healing, I hope to present an overview of some of the most important basic contributions NLP has to offer. The NLP modelling process has primarily taken place by contrasting the strategies and behavior of people who have exhibited different degrees of success in responding to physical illness and maintaining health. The domain of NLP exploration is defined by the situation in which two patients show the same symptoms, are diagnosed as having the same illness at equivalent stages. They are given the same prognosis and the same treatment, yet one of them gets better and eventually recovers while the condition of the other worsens or does not improve. In such a case the critical variable must be in the internal neurological and behavioral responses of the individual as the external conditions are basically the same.

The NLP model has also been used to examine the behavior of people who are consistently healthy as compared to people who are chronically ill. NLP maintains that it is in the differences between these strategies that the most important information lies.

It should be pointed out that the primary purpose of this modelling procedure is to add more choices to peoples' abilities to achieve and maintain health not to limit or judge other choices. Many promoters of natural, spiritual or psychological health methods can be as closed-minded as the traditional medical community that they criticize. The strategies and principles that I will be presenting here may be utilized and applied independent of whatever other method is also currently being used. Their function is to enhance the process of health and may be used to promote the effectiveness of any other method.

In addition to definitions and examples, I will help illustrate the application of these principles and strategies as a coherent whole by presenting extracts from a transcript of a one-hour NLP session conducted with a woman (referred to as B) who was in an advanced stage of leukemia and had been hospitalized for the second time. A friend of the patient's (referred to as H) had asked the author to speak with her as she had become increasingly depressed and had given up hope of ever leaving the hospital again. Her friends described her as a "hermit" as she no longer made any attempt to contact or communicate with anyone but a select few. The author's goal was to help her regain enough of her mental and physical capabilities to allow her to function as comfortably and normally as possible, regardless of the course of her treatment or her illness.

A. The Mechanics of "Positive Attitude."

One of the most commonly identified features of people who are successful at maintaining their health is that of a "positive attitude." And yet, while people agree that this is an important aspect of health, they also agree that you cannot just simply tell someone to "get a positive attitude." Using NLP modelling principles, however, one can identify a number of features and processes that seem to characterize the mechanics of achieving a positive attitude such that a person can take specific steps to attain one.

1. Outcome Versus Problem Orientation

Perhaps the most obvious feature of people who have a "positive attitude" is that they focus on their goals or desired outcomes as opposed to their current problems or all of the things that could go wrong. The question, "What will it be like when you are fully healthy and recovered?" will elicit a completely different response than the question, "How are you broken?" Many people's orientation towards achieving health is to accomplish it by *avoiding* problems and symptoms rather than having a representation of physical health that they can move towards. Often, thinking of a situation you are trying to avoid can actually lead you into having the experience you were attempting to escape. For example, if I said,

"Avoid paying attention to your breathing as you read this sentence," you may find that your response is to automatically pay attention to it in order to merely understand the words.

There is an old tale about a genie who reveals the whereabouts of a treasure chest to a young adventurer. The genie tells the adventurer that he may open the chest and have all its contents so long as he doesn't think of the color blue as he is opening it. If he does think of the color blue, a horrible fate will befall him. As the young man is opening the box he reminds himself not to think of blue—but, of course, in the act of thinking about what *not* to think about, he foils himself.

Since most of modern medical training revolves around the identification and remediation of physical problems and ailments, it is often difficult for professionals in the medical community to orient towards an outcome frame (a medical student's typical introduction to his profession, in fact, is through the study of a cadaver). Often the medical concept of health seems to be the absence of problems. (It is interesting to note that the pervasiveness of this approach in our society is even evident in our educational system. Many times a perfect performance on a test is scored as "−0" instead of "+100." Again, such an orientation is towards avoiding mistakes rather than achieving goals.)

Remembering to keep an orientation toward the desired state can have an important impact. The author once accompanied a woman recovering from breast cancer to see her oncologist in order to help her gather information about a treatment he was proposing. The author asked the doctor how they would know when the woman would be ready to stop taking the treatment. The well-intentioned doctor thought for a moment and then replied, "When it stops working." Although the doctor didn't realize it, the presuppositions of his answer may have been quite devastating.

A good example of the contrast between the different types of attitude was in the behavior of a man the author worked with who had Parkinson's disease. The man had been quite successful in business but had a difficult time with his physical health. The author noticed almost immediately that whenever the man talked about his health he used a negative orientation. When the author asked the man how he would be if he could attain his health, the man would respond, "Well, I *wouldn't* feel so stiff and my joints *wouldn't* ache. I *wouldn't* feel so tired . . ." He always responded by identifying what he *wouldn't* be experiencing. When asked to describe a time when he had successfully accomplished something in his life, the man described how he had cured himself of a phobia of flying. He related how he had used self-hypnosis and had visualized the entire plane trip going perfectly. He visualized being perfectly calm and comfortable and enjoying himself the whole flight. This strategy of orienting toward the outcome had worked beautifully for him.

The author pointed out this difference in thinking to the man and asked him how he thought of his current illness. The man said he had never really thought of it but that he had been told that a part of his brain had died. The author questioned him further about his internal representation of his brain, asking whether he visualized this as meaning that a piece of his brain had "turned black and withered up," had shrunk in size, or merely become inactive.

He was also directed to visualize what his brain, body and behavior would look like if it were functioning perfectly normally and healthily. As the man began to explore his own representations of his situation he realized that he had been limiting his own view of himself and began to experience new hope about his recovery. This change in orientation, or attitude, marked a dramatic shift in his responses to his therapy, treatments and to himself. He has since been able to regain freedom and ease of movement which have remained to the time of this writing.

2. Feedback Versus Failure Orientation

Another important characteristic of positive attitude is the ability to perceive and incorporate an unsuccessful attempt at achieving an outcome as feedback rather than a failure. If an unsuccessful attempt is used as feedback then the information gained by making the attempt may be used to find other choices or to discover how, specifically, the attempt didn't work and thus pinpoint what needs to be changed, added or deleted, in order for the attempt to work. If the unsuccessful attempt is perceived as failure, then one can only look for where to place the blame: "it was the treatment's fault," "it was the doctor's fault," "the patient is incapable of recovery," etc. One common result of failure orientation is that a person tries a particular tack once and if they are unsuccessful will reject the entire approach ("I've tried that already and it doesn't work") rather than look for what might need to be changed in order to make it work.

The human body is an incredibly complex interconnected system that is subject to many influences coming from the environment, activity of the immune system, attitude, individual neurological strategies and personality characteristics, subtle changes in body chemistry, nutrition, and so on. A small change in any one of these influences can tip the physiological "scales" in either direction. Changing any one of these variables and trying the same approach again can make a tremendous difference in the results. Many professionals have a tendency to view things through the filter of their own expertise. A micro biologist will tend to recommend a chemical approach, a surgeon will recommend surgery, a radiologist will recommend radiation, a nutrition specialist will tend to recommend a nutritional approach. Often the research methods used to study a certain approach completely ignore one or a number of possible critical influences. In NLP we believe that all possible choices and resources should be considered. Health is not "caused" by NLP or a positive attitude, these are rather organizing principles that will help a person find choices and take full advantage of the physical, environmental, nutritional, chemical, and behavioral potentials around him or her, in addition to whatever direct physiological influence they may have via the individual's neurology. People who are successful at being healthy do not limit the scope of their resources to finding "the right way" but rather take advantage of all of the potential influences available that may help them to reach their outcome.

Many of the principles we have discussed thus far are illustrated in the first portion of the transcript with the patient. Notice how easily she slips into both problem and failure orientation.

Transcript

MAN: The best place to start is to find out if you have something specific that you want. We have a model of behavior that was built by observing people who do things well: from communicating, to being healthy, to being creative. And most of what I have to offer would be specific strategies or observations about health that I know have worked for other people. Every person is different and has his own unique and particular thinking styles and personal history, but what we've done is to find people who have been able to do amazing things, good things—do things well—and discover how specifically they did it. And I guess H has probably talked to you about some ways in which to organize your experience—talking to parts of yourself, using certain kinds of imagery or things like that. They are patterns that we discovered in successful people and teach to other people in similar situations, and that seem to be really effective. I can offer you a backlog of experience and help you with some strategies for getting healthy. I know that, for instance, in going over some of the things that H said, that you talked about having to struggle a lot—wanting to do things and finding it difficult to do them. Those are things that I can offer you strategies for and make a lot easier. In other words, you don't have to experience things as a struggle. In terms of the specifics, your symptoms, one of the things that we found is that a lot of times by teaching you the strategies of people who have been in a position such as yours and have gotten better, you can accomplish the same thing. Part of what we can do

Applications of NLP in Health

is to tailor the strategies to you as a unique individual. So, if there is something that you would like specifically or something that would help you out, now is the time to ask.

WOMAN: Well, obviously, I definitely want to be healthy (eyes move down and left). There's no *question* about it. I went for a second opinion about my treatment, and this doctor amazed me tremendously, because he *told* me that the most important thing is mental attitude. But this is not what my doctor is *saying*. And I found it very difficult to believe that my attitude could get better (eyes move down and right). Although I found it very easy to believe that my attitude could get worse.

MAN: How do you feel that your attitude could get worse?

WOMAN: I already have leukemia (eyes down right). So, no matter how much whole wheat I eat, or vitamin C's I take I don't think it's going to get better. But now I'm thinking (eyes down and left)—there's always something in the back of my mind—and I'm *saying:* "I'm going to recover." In today's paper, they had Jacque Dembwa's article about his two-year-old son. When his son had cancer, they all thought he was going to die. The child didn't die. So, I think it's a question of having a mental attitude to be okay and not question it (eyes down right). Instead, I *feel,* who am I that I should be the one out of seven million people who's going to stay around?

MAN: Part of it is finding out what people do who are one out of seven million, then you can start to make ten and then twenty. That's what medical science is all about. In other words, as you say, whole wheat and vitamin C might not help, but maybe something else will. Just saying to yourself, "I'm going to get better," may not be all that it takes. But other things that you can do can help to make you well. So part of it has to do with finding the right things to do. In that sense, there are certain kinds of attitudes that are not going to make a difference if they're not complete. Just saying to yourself, "I'm going to be healthy", in itself is not enough, though it may make a difference. It's got to involve the whole person. Part of my beliefs involve the fact that, to me, thinking is a set of events that take place in the brain. When somebody makes a picture in his mind, it is really not a picture. It's a neurological process, and your brain is part of the body. It controls your body. So, very definitely, when someone thinks of a time when he was really scared, you'll see his heart beats faster and his breathing alters and it affects his body very much. So you can tell that an attitude is not always an amorphous thing. It's a very solid, physical activity.

B. Motivation Strategies

The reader will no doubt have noticed that B's responses include an indication of the direction her eyes moved as she spoke. This is because this information can give much insight into her thinking strategies. Of particular interest here is B's motivational strategy. As we pointed out earlier, the strategies we have developed will control many aspects of the way we learn, structure our beliefs and organize our experience. Many strategies, however, are to a large degree unconscious and it would be disruptive to attempt to make a patient aware of them. Through observation and research the developers of NLP have identified ways to read people's strategies independent of their conscious awareness. This is primarily accomplished through the observation of an individual's "accessing cues." As we pointed out in *NLP Vol. I:*

Accessing cues are behaviors that we develop to tune our bodies and affect our neurology in such a way that we can access one representational system more strongly than the others. Just as we prepare to execute any overt behavior independently from the other choices available to us, like jumping, laughing, running or talking, by flexing our muscles and changing our breathing rates and eye scanning patterns in the specific ways that single out that behavior from all others, we operate similarly with cognitive behavior and complex internal processing. Each of us must systematically cycle through specific and recurrent behavioral cues to perform our strategies ... There are two principal ways which we have found effective in teaching people in our training seminars to refine their ability to detect representational systems:

(1) attending to accessing cues which may be detected visually. Specifically (for the right-handed person):

accessing cue	representational system indicated	
eyes up and to the left	eidetic imagery	(V)
eyes up and to the right	constructed imagery	(V)
eyes defocused in position	imagery	(V)
eyes down and to the left	internal dialogue	(A)
telephone positions	internal dialogue	(A)
eyes left or right, same level of gaze	internal auditory	(A)
eyes down and to the right	body sensations	(K)
hand(s) touching on midline	body sensations	(K)

(2) attending to the choice of predicates selected (typically, unconsciously) by the client to describe his experience (see *Patterns, Volume I,* pages 68–76, 82–86 and *The Structure of*

Magic, Volume II, part I). When describing experiences, each of us selects words to describe the portions of experience we attend most closely to. Thus, as communicators, when we train ourselves to detect which representational system is presupposed by the words selected by our clients to describe their experience, we have information which we can utilize effectively in our communication with them.

These are, of course, only two ways of learning to detect representational systems—there are many others.

The predicates chosen by B that indicate a specific representational system have been italicized in the transcript.

Putting together the information indicated by B's verbal and non-verbal responses, it seems that she tends to flip back and forth between her auditory (hearing) and kinesthetic (feeling) representational systems. In one verbalization she indicates that one doctor "told" her that attitude was the most important thing but that she feels her's can only get worse. In the next verbalization she first indicates that she doesn't feel her health will improve, but finds herself telling herself she will recover, only to end up feeling unworthy of recovery.

This preliminary evaluation seems to indicate that B's positive orientation is prompted by an internal voice, while her negative orientation comes from her kinesthetic representational system. Note how the author has incorporated and paced B's representational system predicates in his responses to her. In the last two sentences of the previous transcript section the author has attempted to pace and lead both the voice and the feelings to a positive orientation, especially the feelings ("It's a very *solid* physical activity").

In the next section of the transcript the author

elicits and explores B's motivational strategy in more detail. The usefulnes of this information is two-fold; (1)if the author needs to help motivate B or present information to her in such a way that she will be maximally responsive to it, he can present it to her in a form that is most consistent with her motivational strategy; (2)if the structure of B's motivational strategy is contributing to her difficulties in responding creatively to her situation, then a new one may be designed and installed.

MAN: Now, I am not a doctor and do not pretend to be. All that I can do is help you change things up here, in your mind, which when done in an appropriate way can make a strong impact. You see, your mind and body are part of the same system. You breathe because your brain tells you how fast to. You know how to move because your brain functions to tell you how to move. When you get tired and have a poor attitude, you tend to get sicker more easily. Stress control is a very commonly known phenomenon that shows how close a relationship there is between what you think and what happens physically. Our research has been to explore out how far we can extend that relationship by finding people who have had the experience of regaining health under difficult circumstances—not making guesses about it; not just saying it for the sake of saying it—but to find people who really have helped themselves physically and model their strategies. I do not have any set of magic words. But the thing that I think would be the most useful to you, in any event, is to help you get over some of that struggle because it may not affect only your attitude about your illness, it may come up in all aspects of your life. If you were to characterize it, just as a start, what would you say? What kinds of struggles do you have? Why don't we start with this particular issue of your health?

WOMAN: (Eyes down right) I *feel* guilty so many times, because I'm not really out with the world and, given a choice, this is not what I really want to do. I mean I could live very happily on a Greek island.

MAN: How about doing things to help yourself too? Things that you could be doing that you're not doing?

WOMAN: (Eyes down right) I did some mental exercises that were supposed to help my sickness, but I find it so boring. And I really did try to visualize some parts of the body, but, I find it so *boring*. And then, you know, you're also supposed to mentally go to some place where you are physically in good health. M *told* me you do not have to stay long, but believe me I went everywhere. It is boring because you're doing these things three times a day. It seems to me, once you get in *touch* with something and it *says*, like mine *tells* me, to *see* things in another way, you don't have to keep *asking*.

MAN: Did you begin to see things in another way?

WOMAN: I started a little bit.

MAN: Uh hm.

WOMAN: M helped me in that (eyes down left) she *told* me you have to *look* at how you *CAN see* things, before you can look at them in other ways (eyes down right). But, then once one does that, and believe me it is not that I am doing anything

Applications of NLP in Health

else, I just find that I do not know if I want to *talk* to anyone else, well, I mean to all these other parts. Like, you see, three times a day is too much.

MAN: What kinds of things *do* you like to do? Are there things that would motivate you? Just what would you be happy doing?

WOMAN: (Eyes up left) I would be producing shows, be with my cat and (eyes down right) be where it is *warm*, with my friends.

MAN: How is thinking about your cat or Greece different than thinking about something else?

WOMAN: (Eyes move up left then down right) I *feel* good as if I am fulfilled, but you see I do not want to use the *words* "I *feel* good" and that "all is good in the world."

MAN: What makes you feel those things? I think that has partly to do with how you look at it. When you think of Greece or your cat, you get a feeling and do you get an image too?

WOMAN: (Eyes up left) Oh, I recollect all the times I was there.

MAN: When you recollect them, do you see it as if you were there, or do you see yourself in the picture? In other words, there are two possible ways to look at it. I could be seeing myself over there doing something, or I could be there, seeing it as I have already seen it.

WOMAN: Sometimes one way, sometimes the other way.

MAN: Would either of them make you just as excited?

WOMAN: Well, to use M's method, (eyes down left), you would have to be as if you were actually there, you would have to go there and be there.

MAN: Well, to me, you do different ones for different things and both are very important. What I want to find out now is, when you think of things, you really like to do, which one is it? For example, if you were to think of Greece what would you see?

WOMAN: (Eyes up left) I would be there.

MAN: O.K. How about with your cat?

WOMAN: (Eyes up left) Oh definitely.

MAN: You'd be there?

WOMAN: Yes.

MAN: O.K. And how about producing a show?

WOMAN: (Eyes up left) Absolutely.

MAN: So, when you think of those things you actually see how it would occur from your own perspective?

WOMAN: Yes, I think so.

MAN: Now, when you think about doing those exercises, how do you think of them?

WOMAN: (Eyes down left) I think that I have to do it.

MAN: So what is different, is it that you hear the words, "I have to," or something different about the words?

WOMAN: (Eyes down left) Well, it is good for me.

MAN: But at this moment when you think about doing them you are not motivated to do them?

WOMAN: (Eyes down right) Oh, definitely not.

… Applications of NLP in Health

MAN: O.K. Now, if I say, "Do you want to come to Greece?"

WOMAN: (Eyes up left then down right) Ha. Ha.

MAN: You would say "yes." In that case you didn't tell yourself you had to, but you actually saw being there?

WOMAN: Well probably. It was fast, because when I like doing something, I don't have that drag as when I don't.

The information gathered in this last section of the transcript has added another dimension to B's motivational strategy. It seems that the things that B is most motivated to do are stored and triggered visually. And, while B's internal voice is trying to get her to do things that are good for her, by telling herself that she "has to" or "should" do something she elicits a reactionary response in her feelings. B's motivational problems seem to occur in the linkage between her auditory representational system and her kinesthetic representational system.

If one would want to communicate to B in the most resourceful and compelling manner, then, one would want to lead visually — particularly with associated imagery (first person point of view).

C. Congruence

Perhaps the most important aspect of achieving a healthy state is personal congruence. A person is "congruent" when all of his internal processes and behavior are fully in agreement and oriented toward securing a desired outcome. This is often difficult to do with physical problems. Notice how B demonstrates a number of consistent incongruencies in her statements. As soon as she tells herself she "has to" or "should" do something that she thinks is good for her she begins to feel that she doesn't want to do it. It sounds good, but doesn't feel right.

In NLP the concept of "parts" is used as a metaphor to describe the interaction between different strategies or programs of behavior. People develop varying strategies and programs for different functions like creativity, motivation and evaluation. Sometimes the results of two or more of an individual's strategies will conflict or are incongruent with one another. A particular program of behavior can tend to take on a persona which becomes identified as a part of the person. For example, it is common to hear people describe an incongruency with words like, "one part of me wants to do the things that I see are good for me, but then another part just keeps telling me that I can 'put it off.' " If a person is not congruent, he will often appear to be sabotaging his own needs and wants.

NLP extends the metaphor of "parts" by having people literally talk to parts of themselves. It is not that the model of NLP considers there to be actual little people running around inside of somebody's head making him do things; rather it is a convenient and naturally occurring way to assist people in separating, identifying, accessing and organizing programs of behavior. "Reframing" is an NLP technique that provides a set of steps through which people may contact parts of themselves and negotiate with those parts in order to achieve internal harmony and congruence (see *Frogs Into Princes*, Bandler and Grinder, 1979 and *Roots of NLP*, Dilts, 1983).

1. Adaptive Intention of Behavior

In NLP all behavior is believed to have been established for an adaptive purpose or positive intention. Any behavior, no matter how useless, crazy or detrimental it may appear, is believed to be the best choice available to the person exhibiting it at that point in time. If the individual is given a better choice that satisfies the same intention that the problematic behavior satisfies, the individual will naturally incorporate that choice into his repertoire of behavior.

While consulting for a mental health clinic, the author was asked to do an hour session with a woman who was alcoholic and depressed to the point of being suicidal (both alcoholism and depression are believed by many to stem from physical causes). The author asked the woman if she could contact the part of herself that caused her to drink. The part was characterized by a particular feeling in her stomach area. She was then asked to go inside and ask the part responsible for her drinking what it was trying to do for her by making her drink. She responded by saying that the part of her indicated it was trying to kill her. Since this did not seem very adaptive, the author explored the intention further by having the woman ask the part of herself what it was trying to do positively for her by wanting to kill her. She responded that it said it was trying to get her peace. When the author asked, "Peace from what, specifically?" the woman shifted her eyes down and to her left and said, "I don't know." By having observed her eye movement, however, the author was able to determine that it was most likely an internal voice. (It is interesting to note that most depressed people tend to keep their eyes down left and down right and very rarely look up or access visually. These accessing cues are indicative of the negative auditory—kinesthetic loops that can easily make people depressed.) The author instructed the woman to keep her eyes down and left and pay attention to whatever was going on in her mind. The woman was somewhat suprised when she discovered a voice, lingering just outside of her conscious awareness, that was constantly criticizing her and telling her that she was a bad person. When the author asked whose voice it was, the woman realized that it belonged to her mother, who had constantly criticized her as a child. Because the voice had never been in her awareness, the woman had never learned to deal with it and had only felt the effects of her response. It seemed that her only choices for shutting it off were to drink herself into an altered state of consciousness where she couldn't feel the effects or by killing herself!

Now that her internal voice was conscious, the author had the woman ask it what it was trying to do for her by constantly criticizing her and calling her a "bad girl." The voice replied that it was trying to make her a good person. The author asked the woman to point out to the part that it was actually achieving the exact opposite of what it intended. The more the voice criticized her, the worse she felt and the more she felt the need to drink as a means to avoid the bad feelings and shut off the voice. The more she drank, of course, the more critical the voice would become later, which would restart the cycle. The author then had the woman ask the internalized voice of her mother if, since its intention was to help her become a better person, it would be willing to try some different choices to motivate the woman to change her behavior. The part agreed and the rest of the session was spent conditioning the voice to alter its tone, tempo and verbal patterns (like using an outcome orientation as opposed to the critical negative orientation) so that its effect would be less painful and more effective. The change immediately relieved much of the unnecessary pressures the woman had been experiencing in her life and allowed her to make the other changes she desired in her life with much greater ease.

Some typical sources of incongruency with regard to health that may need to be reframed stem from (1) beliefs about the relationship between mind and body and one's ability to affect one's own physiology, (2) attempts to avoid false hope by not having hope at all, (3) differences in opinions between professionals and one's own assessment of one's physical state.

A woman with whom the author worked had a sudden stroke in her early 70s, even though she was in very good health. While discussing ways to use NLP to treat some of the problems that had arisen as a result of the stroke, a part of the woman surfaced that indicated that a person whom the woman had admired and modelled herself after had died at the age she had reached at that time. The part of her felt that if she lived longer than this person she had loved and respected it would be an insult to him in that it would be as if she were trying to better him or "one-up" him. The part was reframed and the woman, in her 80's at the time of this writing, has had no further problems with strokes.

A man with liver cancer, who came to consult with the author, discovered a part of himself that didn't want him to recover. It seems that a group of his friends had gotten together and thrown a party for him in which everyone had bared his soul and faced his own mortality. The whole group grew closer together because of this experience and had all said a tearful goodbye to their "dying" friend. The man was so touched by the experience that a part of him felt he would let his friends down if he recovered. The party was such a peak experience for him that he was afraid his survival would not measure up in comparison. Naturally, this part was immediately reframed.

Often, where an illness is hereditary, an individual will have a part of him that believes he should follow in the footsteps of his other family members out of respect. One effective way to reframe this is by having the person look back at the family members he or she loved and respected and watch as each follows the tradition or pattern of the illness, remembering how he or she had learned so much from them. The individual is then instructed to look forward and visualize his or her children or family watching the individual with respect and anticipation as a respected model for their own behavior. This will immediately put the pattern into a new perspective.

a. Secondary Gain

Secondary gain is well known among psychological professionals as a phenomenon in which some seemingly negative, unhealthful or self-destructive behavior is actually achieving something that the patient wants at a different level as a positive by-product. Smoking, for instance, is a habit that appears to be self-destructive and serve no positive physiological purpose. Yet the behavior of smoking can have a number of positive secondary effects such as allowing the smoker to relax, fit into a particular social image or, paradoxically enough, even to remind the person to breathe when he or she is in a tense situation. If the individual attempts to extinguish or change the behavior without supplying other choices through which the same positive by-products may be achieved, then any attempt to change the behavior will be painful or hindered by the incongruency created by the loss of the resource.

It is obvious that the phenomenon of secondary gain in illness and the concept of positive intention are very closely related. Illness may cause a number of positive secondary effects ranging from getting attention or sympathy to having a good excuse for taking a break or avoiding work, tests or other negative situations. One woman with whom the author worked had developed a pattern of getting seriously ill because as a child she had been sexually abused by her father while her mother stood by passively. She would become so afraid of her father that she wouldn't be able to breathe and would start wheezing. Apparently her mother interpreted the labored breathing to mean that she was enjoying the experience and would punish the girl later for leading her father on. The only way out of this bizarre home life for the girl was when she became so seriously ill that she had to go to the hospital, which, even as an adult, was her equivalent for comfort and safety. The problem arose when, after the woman had left home, the pattern continued whenever she was in a stressful situation or began to get into a close relationship. She had even been thought to be terminally ill by doctors on three separate occasions. This difficulty was dealt with by negotiating with her parts to create new resources and choices for handling her adult circumstances.

b. Illness as Communication

Responding to illness as a communication allows one to locate and treat the cause rather than the symptom. When our bodies deviate from a healthy state it is a communication to us that some action needs to be taken. The ability to respond to illness or a physical problem as a communication can lead us to resources and choices that are not available if we perceive it as something bad that is always a foreign invader. For example, I struggled with acne for many years, trying many different medicines and creams to treat the blemishes, until I realized that the pimples were not a negative symptom or illness. On the contrary, the pimple was the appropriate healthy reaction of the body in response to body chemistry changes brought about by diet, stress level and self-image. From that point onward I stopped using any medication, which was merely treating the symptom, and responded to the blemishes as a communication about diet and stress. The acne cleared up almost immediately and my skin has remained healthier than when I was taking medication. When blemishes do occasionally appear they are now a communication to me about some steps to take to change things that are under my control as opposed to being some illness or disease that is in control of me.

Another good example of responding to a physical problem as a communication also comes from my own personal history. For about four years, as a young adult, I had been consistently bothered by a cyst at the base of my spine (similar to a small open sore). I had consulted two different doctors on the matter and both had said that the only way to eliminate it was to have it surgically removed, a painful process that would involve the patient being off of his feet for close to six weeks. Naturally, I was not enthused by the prospect. When I began learning about NLP, I tried the process of reframing to contact with the part responsible for the cyst to find out what it was communicating. The response of the part was quite simple. It said I needed to learn more about my body and begin a regular exercise program. After this, I realized that even though I had been bothered by this cyst for four years I had no idea of what it looked like. It was as if it were a dark hidden place on my body. It was in a spot that was not easily accessible visually and I had always avoided touching it or thinking about it. I began to refine my representations of it, started an exercise program and focussed on improving my personal hygiene. Within three weeks the cyst had completely cleared up. Where before there had been a running sore, there was not even an indentation. It has not returned or bothered me again in five years.

It should be noted that not all communications from parts are in regard to personal change. There have been a number of times when I have asked a part what it was trying to communicate and have gotten back the response, "Go see a doctor," to which I have congruently responded. Our purpose here is simply to get people to start to think of their bodies' processes as something they can be in communication with and in control of rather than as something that controls them. We have found that having a person perceive their illness as a communication can be very useful, especially in systemic disorders, including cancer. Many people who have cancer are so afraid of it that they have a difficult time accepting it as a communication or as having a positive intention, but once they look inside themselves they often make many discoveries and find many new choices and potential for hope. In my experience, a disorder like cancer is generally a communication about the need to make a large scale adjustment in personality or life circumstances. Often it occurs at a critical juncture in a person's life and is typically indicative of serious incongruency in the person's responses to such a change.

2. Feedback

One potential source of personal incongruency is a lack of specific feedback regarding the physical change or goal one is trying to achieve. Patients are often not shown the specific results of their tests so that they can get specific details of their progress as feedback. Feedback is essential to the achievement of success, whether it comes from external tests or a person's own internal assessment. Establishing some means of feedback is essential. When feedback is provided, the results can be astounding.

I have personally spent much time experimenting with and developing biofeedback mechanisms. An associate of mine was involved in a recent project in which military personnel who were to be sent to duty

Applications of NLP in Health

in Alaska were given biofeedback training for temperature in their hands to help them adapt to the cold. They were all trained to increase the temperature of their hands to help with their work. The trainees were all successful in raising the temperature of their hands, some over ten degrees. Of interest, however, is the fact that when the group arrived in Alaska, they thought the experiment had failed because their hands got cold, until they made temperature readings and found that the spot exactly beneath where the temperature sensor was placed was the appropriate temperature. In other words, each of the trainees had unwittingly learned to control his or her temperature to such a degree that they were heating a single spot in their hand!

Lack of feedback for some physical symptoms can be quite problematic. One of the big problems with cancer is that one doesn't know if what one is doing has worked or not, typically, until it is too late. Establishing a means of feedback other than the symptoms, in such cases, is of extreme importance. For instance, the author once worked with a woman who had been diagnosed as having cervical cancer. She wished to avoid surgery, however, and came to see the author to help find other choices that she might utilize to see if she could change her condition before her surgery date. After making the appropriate congruency checks and adjustments, the woman felt that her body was not trying to hurt her and that she could recover, but wanted some form of feedback in order to be sure. The author noted that she had a wart on one of her hands and suggested that she could use some non-critical response at the cellular level, like her wart, as a feedback device. The suggestion was made, among other possibilities, that as her cervical tissue returned to a healthy state so could her wart. The woman forgot about the suggestion for a couple of weeks until one day she noticed that the wart had disappeared. When she went to the doctor, her tests showed that her cervical cancer had also cleared up and she was able to forego surgery.

In the next segment of the transcript, notice how B's congruency issues keep coming up as her various parts become more and more defined. Also note how the author continues to apply the principles of outcome and feedback orientation. Notice also how the author continues to develop and use the information that has been gathered about B's strategies.

MAN: What would you most like to spend your time doing?

WOMAN: (Eyes up left) Producing shows.

MAN: When you say "producing shows," how do you do that? What does it mean?

WOMAN: (Eyes up left) It means having a program in a college; having professional people. And actually the president of the college took me out to dinner before I got sick and he was very eager to start a program.

MAN: One thing I noticed is that the exercises are supposed to give you a good attitude, but if they become boring they are not giving you a good attitude and defeat the purpose. It seems to me that, whether or not the thing that you're working at is "good for you," it still feels better to feel good, independent of what is going to be of value to you. I would agree with you, if the stuff is boring you, it is not of good to you. So I would like to ask, if

Applications of NLP in Health

you were the way you wanted to be right now what would you look like?

WOMAN: Right now? (Eyes up left, then down right) I would just *look* the way I was before getting sick. I just really *felt* wonderful.

MAN: How would you be moving if you were going to see yourself a week from now?

WOMAN: (Eyes up left and right) I would be awake, my *voice* would come back. And I just would get on the telephone immediately and get started with some of my ideas, *talk* to the people I have to *talk* to (eyes down left). After this, I would go back and do all the things I have to. In fact, I really had some fantastic ideas; almost anyone of them *sounds* good. (Eyes up left) I am sure I can *see* that they come to pass.

MAN: O.K. now, I have a question. Is there any part of you that would object to that? It is sort of interesting that you mention the phone. I once worked with a man who was a business consultant and he had an illness that was causing him to go paralyzed. Because of this, he slurred his words a little bit. One of the things that he found was that he could be doing a lot that could really make himself *feel better* by using the phone. But he didn't want to talk to people because he thought they would think he sounded funny. And I asked him about it and he realized he was preventing himself from doing all the stuff that would help him. You know, things that would help him *improve* and *feel better*, he really thought his slight lisp was funny. When he realized this, he started *calling people up* all the time. It was really a whole turnaround. So the question I would ask you now is, are there any things that would stop you from calling those people you mentioned?

WOMAN: The only thing that stops me is the fact that I am in the hospital.

MAN: Well, you could at least set up the appointments.

WOMAN: Yes, but I set up loads of things and I just can't ever keep them. (Eyes down left) I did have some ideas and I did *call* people while I was still in the hospital. They were interested and *said* that they would *call*. But it is not enough for me to *call* up and *say,* "well how about it?" (Eyes down right) It is just my *energy.* As long as I am incapacitated in some way I can't get it started.

MAN: You've gotten yourself in what we call a double bind. You know, "If I could start these things it would make me better, but I can't start them until I feel better."

WOMAN: Exactly. When I am ready to start I end up back in the hospital.

MAN: Is there a part of you that doesn't want you to start?

WOMAN: (Eyes down left) No, in fact I would like to be back there.

MAN: Then I'd say that is something you can do.

WOMAN: If I could, (eyes down right) but I am very lazy.

MAN: So, you are lazy.

WOMAN: (Eyes down right) I am very lazy.

MAN: Yes, well, that is an important piece. If you

Applications of NLP in Health

were to say, "I can produce some really wonderful shows," you could help build up a helpful positive attitude, wanting to be out doing things. Now the thing is if you got lazy, what would happen to stop that? How do you get lazy?

WOMAN: Well the only thing that would stop me is (eyes down left then down right) I would *have* to do it. (Eyes down left) I guess there's no reason I couldn't do it.

MAN: Is something stopping you?

WOMAN: (Eyes down right then glancing around the room) You see seven million people come in and they put the stuff here and here.

MAN: What stops you from telling them, "Put it there?"

WOMAN: (Eyes down right) I *feel* like a victim in this, totally passive.

MAN: Do you want to feel that way?

WOMAN: I think maybe I do, (eyes down right) because how else am I going to live through it?

MAN: Well, I'll tell you, when that consultant picked up the phone, he was not a victim anymore. You know, he began to tell the staff what and what not to do. How would you like to be? How would you want it to be if you could be the way you *want* to be in this situation?

WOMAN: (Eyes down left) No, no. It is the way I *have* to be now.

MAN: That is the place that you come back to consistently. You are motivated to do something because you see that you *want* to do it, not because you *have* to. You don't do things just because you feel guilty if you don't, you do them because that is what you really want to do.

WOMAN: That is correct.

MAN: And I think that is a big part of it, because one of the things I've noticed is that you keep finding out all the reasons something couldn't be that way, or this way. Of course, to take the next step is to find out how we can get your outcomes anyway. Like I say, maybe a couple of words to the people who come in would keep the place a little neater.

WOMAN: *See,* (eyes down right) but I also have the fear that half the time I don't know what is supposed to be happening. I am not used to the hospital yet, you know, I am just starting to get used to it. The first time I was in for thirty-five days, I didn't believe I was sick and did not accept the fact that there was an illness. It wasn't till the second time I was here (eyes down left), that I *told* myself, "I have something wrong with me. It is not just a fluke, or a dream, and that when I wake up I'll find it was a nightmare." When I am working I don't *feel* in such a state (eyes down right). But here I am a victim.

MAN: So part of you feels like a victim. The other part keeps telling you that you have to get going and do all these things.

WOMAN: Yes, absolutely.

MAN: But what you really *want* to be doing is producing shows.

WOMAN: (Eyes up left) Yes, and I did have all those wonderful ideas and I did *speak* to a few people. (Eyes down right) The *feeling* that I got was so strong, you know I could definitely *tell* that my

Applications of NLP in Health

voice was coming back. I could *speak* without hesitating.

MAN: Do you have a good way to tell if you are doing something because you want to?

WOMAN: (Eyes down right) When I'm doing it because I want to, then I have a lot of *energy*. When I am doing it because I am supposed to I get very *tired*.

MAN: Now, you really want to do this project. What would stop you?

WOMAN: (Eyes down left) Well when I couldn't *talk*. (Eyes down right) Also I get *tired* and even now my *voice* is not tremendous. Also you know, not getting out of this place. I experience it as a *struggle*.

MAN: I know H helped you to talk to one of your parts. But sometimes the most important thing to do isn't to talk to just one part, but to negotiate between two that are fighting.

WOMAN: (Eyes down right) Sometimes I *feel* just as if I've been walking on the street and picked up and taken away since this happened to me.

MAN: Do all your parts think that?

WOMAN: No, (Eyes down left) but just now people are just starting to *talk* to me about other things. You know I would get telephone *calls* and nobody would *talk* to me except about having leukemia. But I just wasn't myself anymore. Everyone just forgot I was a person before this happened. (Eyes down right) But I would like a way out of this, because I have a *feeling* of a wet blanket holding me down.

MAN: Yeah, that is some of the sense that I've got.

If you were to make an image of the part of you that is a victim, the one that is lazy, and put it on this hand, what would you see?

D. Visualization

The process of visualization has often been associated with the ability to achieve and maintain health. While it is only one of the five possible senses that could be used to contribute to health, it seems to be the process of choice by many of the people who were modelled for their strategies for health.

The actual physical relationship between the act of visualizing and its' physiological effect is unknown, although, as I pointed out earlier, it is possible for activity in the brain to influence our physiology directly through neural connections. Recent studies have shown that subjects who used visualization procedures while in light self-hypnotic states produced significant measurable increases in their number of white blood cells. The Simontons' method of using visualization to treat cancer patients has become a widely known addition to the choices for dealing with cancer.

The NLP approach to visualization is modelled after these other methods of visualization but incorporates some important differences.

1. Orientation Toward Outcomes, Communication and Congruence

As we pointed out earlier, the people who are the most successful at maintaining their health are those who constantly orient toward their desired outcomes. In addition to creating visual representations of the goal state, NLP promotes an orientation towards integration and balance in that outcome. This is based on the belief that illness is a communication and that all parts and behaviors have an adaptive intention. Rather than have a cancer patient visualize his body as a battleground where good guys and bad guys (in the form of white blood calls and cancer cells) are fighting to the death, the NLP approach would have the person visualize something like a field full of sheep (representing white cells) grazing in the pasture in order to maintain an ecological balance so that the pasture's grass does not grow to the point of being out of hand. Rather than fight one another the NLP approach would have the parts involved in the incongruence negotiate and harmonize with one another.

2. Multi-Level Visualization

There are many different levels at which one may visualize a state of health: at the levels of (a)chemical interactions, (b)cell response, (c)organ function and (d)the overall functioning of the entire body system. In NLP we consider all of these different levels to be important for maintaining health. The typical NLP visualization approach would include having the person visualize a healthy state (either actual or metaphoric) at each of these levels of physiological response.

3. Using All Representational Systems

As we pointed out earlier, the visual system is only one of the sensory resources available to us to help organize our experience. In NLP we strive to have people use all of their senses in conjunction with one another to create representations of their outcome, such as detailed verbal descriptions (auditory) and the feelings of health as well. The more the brain senses an outcome the easier it will be to achieve it. This also helps to avoid incongruencies that may be brought about by a situation in which something may LOOK good but doesn't FEEL right, and so on.

E. Metaphor

The metaphors that people use to think about their health are as important as the fact that they are visualizing. As with the other mental processes we have discussed in this paper, it should be pointed out that thinking about a metaphor involves the organization of physical brain processes and can create as much response in a person's physiology as stress or drugs.

In NLP metaphors are used in three ways:

1. *to make indirect communications to the patient.* Many times this can allow one to avoid the stress, resistance or negative reaction a patient has to talking about his problems directly. Notice how the author used the metaphor of the man he had worked with who had changed his attitude about contacting his friends, and become more active using the phone, in the last section of the transcript with B. This metaphor was used to help associate the act of using the telephone and taking action with the process of getting better.

2. *to help the patient organize his or her own mental map of the illness.* Metaphors are often an easier

Applications of NLP in Health 45

way for patients to understand and impact their health. In the next transcript segment, the author will be working with B on her own metaphors for understanding her physiological processes.

3. *to help gather information and locate new choices.* Considering an illness as a metaphor itself can often be an interesting way to get insight. NLP identifies a class of idioms, called "organ language," that can also be used to help a patient organize and understand his or her situation. Phrases like "a pain in the neck," "get something off my (back/chest)," "I am dying to get this," etc., offer a rich source of potential insight into possible contributors to health disorders.

At our current point in the transcript the author has begun to have B visualize the two parts of herself that are in conflict. This accomplishes three things: (1) it adds in another representational system to the two conflicting parts, which up until this time have been primarily auditory and kinesthetic respectively, (2) it begins to establish a mode of communication and overlap between separate parts or programs of behavior, (3) it helps to create a metaphorical base on which to understand B's perception of her own situation.

As with many people, B was somewhat surprised by what she saw when she looked inside herself. She saw the kinesthetic, lazy, victimized part of herself as a massive building, similar to the World Trade Center. The part of herself that was constantly trying to get her to do the things she "should" do, B saw as a small energetic doll-like person. The author instructed B to have each part look at the other part, in turn, and describe what each perceived to be the strengths and weaknesses of the other. B noted that the part represented by the big building had great strength but lacked mobility and "vision." The part basically lived up to its metaphorical representation of being a building, big and strong but with no energy or perceptivity. The smaller part was very mobile and energetic but failed to view the "big picture" and lacked "grounding." Notice how accurately these images served as metaphors for her behavior.

After pointing out that each part could greatly benefit from the resources of the other, the author instructed B to ask the parts if they would be willing to combine together to make a third part that was an integration of both of them, such that it had full access to both of their resources. The parts agreed to try. The first step toward the combination involved having B try to visualize the building part of herself as a person. This was done to make it easier to relate to that part as actually being a part of herself. In her first attempt to bring the two images together and integrate them, however, the little energetic part became subsumed by the bigger part and disappeared — again, an appropriate metaphor for what had been happening in B's life. B was instructed to ask the big part if it *intended* to engulf the smaller one. The part said that it didn't mean to overwhelm the smaller one. In fact, the big part wished the little one would get bigger. (It is interesting to consider this metaphor in light of the nature of B's disease, leukemia, which is characterized by the inability of the white cells, the cells that "do what is good for" your body, in a person's immune system to mature.) The big one did not want to get smaller but B did not seem to be able to make the little one bigger. Some necessary resource was missing. Considering that both parts really lacked "vision," a component critical to B's motivational strategy, the author decided to include that aspect as a resource to assist in the integration process.

In the last section of the transcript the author endeavors to help B put together all of her parts into a coordinated strategy which is installed by rehearsing, or "futerpacing" B through the strategy sequence using eye movement leads and metaphor. During this process a couple of new dimensions to B's problematic kinesthetic part surface, but their intentions are also incorporated using the reframing process. The author also takes advantage of the process of communicating with these new "parts" of B to make sure that she has internalized the reframing procedure so that she may continue to use it with herself if some future incongruency should arise.

MAN: What takes something from a vision, a dream, to something that you actually do? You've done that before. You have had vision, what does it take now?

WOMAN: These questions aren't easy to answer, I mean, naturally.

MAN: What makes you wonder? I mean, you've done it before.

WOMAN: (Eyes down left) Only because when I'm sick, I plan everything. I mean he is going to do another bone marrow exam and *tell* me I have to go back to the hospital and I don't want to do this again.

MAN: The thing is that you need plan for that possibility. You anticipate everything. Then you ask yourself how, even if he does say that, you can get things done to be in control and not victimized?

WOMAN: I would like not to be victimized (eyes down right), but my good intentions are overcome by my laziness.

MAN: Is that this big building part, or is that something else? See what is the part of you that gets you depressed and lazy? Have you gotten in touch with that one?

WOMAN: (Eyes down right) I guess not.

MAN: See, that one has a good intention too, though it may be hard to accept at this point. One thing you know about that part is that it can overwhelm your best visions. If you had that one working on *your* side you would really have something powerful. Find that one that makes you depressed. It is the one you really want to know about. Do you know what that one would look like?

WOMAN: (Eyes down right then up right) Like a rat or a mole.

MAN: So, one part of you thinks of it as a rat. You know that can distort what it is doing for you.

WOMAN: (Eyes up right) How about a black veil?

MAN: You can get in touch with that part. That depression you get, is it a feeling? When you experience it, how do you know it is there?

Applications of NLP in Health

WOMAN: (Eyes down right) I know how I *feel*.

MAN: So take that feeling and ask it what is it trying to do positively for you. What does it say?

WOMAN: (Eyes down right) This *sounds* crazy, but it *says* it is trying to get me to act.

MAN: Well that is interesting. That seems like a positive intention. Does it know it is actually stopping you from acting?

WOMAN: (Eyes down right) I don't think it does .... I just *told* it ... it is *quiet*.

MAN: Ask it if it understood.

WOMAN: (Eyes down right) It understands.

MAN: So, since what it really wants to do is to help you act, what ways other than just getting you depressed can it use to motivate you? Go to your creative part and ask it if it can come up with other choices to help motivate you, instead of making you lazy.

WOMAN: It's been trying to get me to act but it's been accomplishing just the opposite.

MAN: At this point. But can you think of any creative ways that you want it to use to motivate you?

WOMAN: (Eyes down right) Well the same way I get depression I can get acceleration.

MAN: O.K. That is one choice.

WOMAN: It seems never to have understood that it was depressing me, you know what I mean.

MAN: It is not uncommon.

WOMAN: (Eyes down right) I can't think of anything else.

MAN: So you can only think of one way to actually make you act. I can help think of two other ways.

One other way to remind you to act could be to use words. This part can give you a verbal signal to act in different ways. Another way is to use a picture like a red flag. Now, go back to the feeling of depression and laziness. Ask it if is it willing to accept those choices. Does it have any objections?

WOMAN: (Eyes down right) No.

MAN: If that part would implement those things consistently, then you would really have something good going.

WOMAN: It is very difficult to accept the depressive part.

MAN: I am not asking you to accept the behavior it has been responsible for in the past, but rather the intention behind the behavior. Instead of getting rid of it, respect its intention and get it on your side as a resource. You must take action under many different circumstances. No matter what happens, take advantage of all the resources that you have. That part never before realized that it was accomplishing the opposite of what it intended. One of the things about parts is that there are a lot of behaviors that got established a long time ago that were effective back then but become obsolete as things change. At some time, being depressed may have been a way to motivate you to take action. You know, "when the going gets tough, the tough get going." For instance, the function of those exercises you mentioned before was to build a good attitude but they stopped doing that, they got boring.

WOMAN: How does one function like this? Let us assume tomorrow I get up, make a phone call, not

Applications of NLP in Health

in this area code, and it takes fifteen minutes to make the call. (Eyes down right) I'll get *tired.*

MAN: So where is the feeling coming from? Pretend you're making the call right now.

WOMAN: So many parts to *ask.* Well, I'll *ask* the part that is stopping me from wanting to persist what it is trying to do.

MAN: And what are some examples of what it might say?

WOMAN: (Eyes down right then down left) It seems very helpful. It *says,* "try again, if no answer, wait till Thursday."

MAN: What is it trying to do by making you wait till Thursday?

WOMAN: (Eyes down left) Keep putting it off.

MAN: What is it trying to do for you by putting it off?

WOMAN: That is an interesting question. See, then it is not such a good thing.

MAN: But, you've got to know it's intention if it doesn't give you the answer you want. If it keeps telling you all the bad things that could happen, ask it, "What are you trying to accomplish by stopping me from doing what I want?" Ask that. What is the positive thing it's doing by putting things off?

WOMAN: Well, I'm not going to *ask* it now. You think I should?

MAN: (Laughs) Sure, this is important. Besides it will be easier if you do it now.

WOMAN: Yeah, but it is not stopping me from doing anything. Why would it want to stop me from doing something I want to do? And it is not because I don't want to do it. I guess I'm just lazy.

MAN: You must go back to the question.

WOMAN: (Eyes down right then down left) Its answer seems very contradictory.

MAN: It can get complicated. And if it gets confusing, I'll help.

WOMAN: To buy something takes me forever. I have to buy a stove and I would *look* for years.

MAN: What if you just bought any stove?

WOMAN: Nothing.

MAN: What makes it so strange to do it on the spur of the moment?

WOMAN: Too fast to do. I must know it is good and will like it better than the old one. (Eyes down left) I keep thinking of putting it off until next week. I just *say* it out of habit.

MAN: The voice, is it a habit?

WOMAN: (Eyes down left) If you got along with one so long why get one now? I will save money and time.

MAN: Is it really saving you money and time?

WOMAN: Money maybe, not time. See, I don't *ask* myself those questions.

MAN: To me it is not any effort to ask them. So many times our habits pass the point of usefulness. What would you rather be saying to yourself?

WOMAN: It is like trying to clean up things. I have a stack of papers. (Eyes down left) And I spend weeks, years, thinking how I should clean it up. I did it when I knew I was coming to the hospital this

Applications of NLP in Health

time. I was just astonished by how much I accomplished. All that wasted energy; it is as if I'm caught between doing and not.

MAN: But, the only thing that has been getting you caught was a habit established by a part of you that didn't know it was accomplishing the opposite of what it intended. Now everytime you say, "put it off," you can just as easily think of how easy it was to do the papers. And you can just add that to what the voice says, so it doesn't put you in a negative direction. The part is trying to help you. Ask the voice if it knows about how easy it was to do the papers.

WOMAN: (Eyes down left) It thinks that is a good thing.

MAN: Since it wants to save you time and get you to act, will it be willing to not automatically put things off?

WOMAN: (Eyes down left) Yes.

MAN: So, for instance, when you're going to be calling these people on the phone, what would it be telling you instead of, "It can wait?"

WOMAN: (Eyes down left) Try again, *call* someone else.

MAN: So pretend it's tomorrow and you're starting to make calls.

WOMAN: What is going to happen is it will take a long time. Except if I *call* H, I could reach her right away if she is home. But I have to *call* somebody long distance, but I can get through it.

MAN: Okay. So do you know of anything that could stop you before you start calling?

WOMAN: What could happen before that? (Eyes down right then down left) If I get *irritated* I might think, "I'll call later instead of now." Although I think that is unlikely, because I always *call* the time I think best to *call*. And when you're *asking* somebody for something it is always best to *call* at the best time. I really don't think it'll be a problem anymore.

MAN: There are a couple of things we talked about I'd like to ask you to keep in mind. One of the parts that has stopped you is a voice and one of them is a feeling. What gets you to do things is the vision of what you want. If at the times when you are waiting, they could remind you to just to keep sight of the vision, then you could use this time to keep it enjoyable. Now, I think both parts of you, if they knew that, would signal you to keep that vision in mind. That vision is the essence of your positive attitude. What happens is you forget about what you're doing the phone calls, or whatever, for. It only becomes a drag if it has no purpose. When people make pictures, the eyes shift up. The eyes would actually shift up this way (points to B's upper left). When people have feelings, the eyes shift down to the right. When they talk to themselves the eyes shift down and left. See, I knew ahead of time you were saying something to yourself, for example, with the part of you that told you to "put it off." On the other hand, when I asked you about the things you liked to do, when you were talking about your visions, you were looking up here. The place you put your eyes actually makes a difference. For instance, we teach kids how to spell by looking up and visualizing the words. The kids who try to look down and left and sound it out have a harder time. When people visualize, the eyes shift up. If you can remember to shift your eyes up and focus on the vision, to focus on the things that you want to do, you will find yourself feeling more energized. Since the feeling's intention is to get you to act anyway, it can *show* you how to do it. It can remind you to *focus* on how you want it to be. See, this is one of the important things we teach in our work. It is also a real big characteristic of people who are able to be healthy. They always focus on the outcome rather than on the problem. The person who thinks about the problem all the time could get real depressed. If you focus on your outcome you are then looking where you are going to. So if something stops it you can turn it around by focussing on your vision of your goal. The picture is the thing that will get you exhilarated. I think the orientation back to where you want to go is very important. Does that sound good to all your parts?

WOMAN: Oh, it *sounds* beautiful, wonderful.

MAN: The important thing is, find how to get back to where you were going.

WOMAN: The point is to take advantage of these things.

MAN: Well, remember the habit of saying, "put it off," developed for positive reasons. The part responsible for that habit will help you take advantage of your new choices because they will help it achieve its intention of saving time and money.

Also remember that there are many things you've learned to do and take advantage of in your life that you didn't have to consciously practice. I believe that a person will learn much easier and faster when new behaviors fit all parts of their personality. If new choices work well, they will be incorporated naturally. All of us do things we didn't start out doing.

As a final resource, I would like to leave you with one of my favorite stories about Albert Einstein. Someone once asked Einstein, "You have spent your life studying the workings of the Universe from the tiny atom to the immensity of the Cosmos. What do you think the most important question is for mankind to find the answer to?" Einstein, in his characteristic fashion, looked up and off into space for a moment and then cast his gaze down at his shoelaces. He then looked back at the man and said, "I think the most important question a person needs to answer for him or herself is, 'Is the universe a friendly place?' If people think the universe is a friendly place then they will know that there is an order to it and that it is geared toward adaptation and they will be constantly looking for its wonders and laws. If people think it is an unfriendly place then they will spend their lives building walls and weapons to protect themselves from the evil they feel is all around them and even inside of them."

I believe that the universe is a friendly place, though not necessarily always safe or perfect. I think that harmony and cooperation are perfectly natural but not always naturally perfect. What I have offered you are some tools that I believe can help you to achieve more harmony and choices in your own life and to creatively surmount the challenges you face. Good bye.

Epilogue

B did make her phone calls the next day, and continued to make them. Her voice and her strength returned and shortly after this session she was released from the hospital. Her friends noticed an immediate and dramatic improvement in her behavior. She was no longer a hermit but instead became a dynamo. She met with the president of the college and managed to secure the money for her production and the professional assistance needed to carry it through the arduous pre-production stages. And, while she made the decision to continue her chemotherapy, she no longer acted or felt sick or weak and remained in good health.

It is unfortunate to have to add, however, that, because her chemotherapy was so intense, it all but disabled B's immune system and lowered her physical defenses. A few months after the session presented here, B caught an infection from a catheter used during the administration of her chemotherapy. Because her body had no natural defense system, the infection spread rapidly and intensely. Within a few days of getting the infection B died, not from her leukemia but her treatment.

GLOSSARY OF NLP TERMINOLOGY

GLOSSARY OF NLP TERMINOLOGY

ACCESSING CUES - Subtle behaviors that will both help to trigger and indicate which representational system a person is using to think with. Typical types of accessing cues include eye movements, voice tone and tempo, body posture, gestures and breathing patterns.

ANCHORING - The process of associating an internal response with some external trigger (similar to classical conditioning) so that the response may be quickly, and sometimes covertly, reaccessed.

AUDITORY - Relating to hearing or the sense of hearing.

BEHAVIORAL FLEXIBILITY - The ability to vary one's own behavior in order to elicit or secure a response from another person.

CALIBRATION - The process of learning to read another person's responses in an ongoing interaction by pairing observable behavioral cues with a specific internal response.

CALIBRATED LOOP - Unconscious pattern of communication in which behavioral cues of one person trigger specific responses from another person in an ongoing interaction.

CONGRUENCE - When all of a person's internal

strategies and behaviors are fully in agreement and oriented toward securing a desired outcome.

DEEP STRUCTURE - The sensory maps (both conscious and unconscious) that people use to organize and guide their behavior.

FOUR-TUPLE (or 4-tuple) - A shorthand method used to notate the structure of any particular experience. The concept of the four tuple maintains that any experience must be composed of some combination of the four primary representational classes - $<A, V, K, O>$ - where A = auditory, V = visual, K = kinesthetic, and O = olfactory/gustatory.

FUTURE PACING - The process of mentally rehearsing oneself through some future situation in order to help insure that the desired behavior will occur naturally and automatically.

GUSTATORY - Relating to taste or the sense of taste.

INCONGRUENCE - Where two or more parts or programs of an individual are in conflict or disagreement. This conflict often leads to the seeming sabatoge of the individual's consciously stated goals.

INSTALLATION - The process of facilitating the acquisition of a new strategy or behavior. A new strategy may be installed through some combination of anchoring, accessing cues, metaphor or futurepacing.

KINESTHETIC - Relates to body sensations. In NLP the term kinesthetic is used to encompass all kinds of feelings including tactile, visceral and emotional.

META MODEL - A model developed by John Grinder and Richard Bandler that identifies categories of language patterns that can be problematic or ambiguous, and provides on inquiry system by which these language patterns may be challenged or enriched.

METAPHOR - The process of thinking about one situation or phenomenon as something else, i.e., stories and analogies.

MODELLING - The process of observing and mapping the successful behaviors of other people.

NEURO-LINGUISTIC PROGRAMMING (NLP) - A behavioral model and set of explicit skills and techniques founded by John Grinder and Richard Bandler in 1975. The model was derived by observing the patterns of excellence in experts from diverse fields of professional communication including psychotherapy, business, hypnosis, law and education.

OLFACTORY - Relating to smell or the sense of smell.

OUTCOMES - Goals or desired states that a person or organization aspires to achieve.

PACING - A method used by communicators to quickly establish rapport by matching certain aspects of their behavior to those of the person with whom they are communicating - a matching or mirroring of behavior.

PARTS - A metaphorical way of talking about independent programs and strategies of behavior. Programs or "parts" will often develop a persona that becomes one of their identifying features.

PREDICATES - Process words (like verbs, adverbs and adjectives) that a person selects to describe a subject. Predicates are used in NLP to identify which representational system a person is using to process information.

QUOTES - A pattern in which a message that you want to deliver can be embedded in quotations, as if someone else had stated the message.

RAPPORT - The establishment of trust, harmony and cooperation in a relationship. In NLP this is primarily accomplished through the process of "pacing."

REFRAMING - A process used in NLP through which a problematic behavior is separated from the positive intention of the internal program or "part" that is responsible for the behavior. New choices of behavior are established by having the part responsible for the old behavior take responsiblilty for implementing other behaviors that satisfy the same positive intention but don't have the problematic by-products.

REPRESENTATIONAL SYSTEMS - The five senses: seeing, hearing, touching (feeling), smelling, and tasting.

REPRESENTATIONAL SYSTEM PRIMACY - Where an individual systematically uses one sense over the other to process and organize his or her experience. Primary representational system will determine many personality traits as well as learning capabilities.

SECONDARY GAIN - Where some seemingly negative or problematic behavior actually carries out some positive function at some other level. For ex-

Golssary of NLP Terms 65

ample, smoking may help a person to relax or help them fit a particular self-image.

STRATEGY - A set of explicit mental and behavioral steps used to achieve a specific outcome. In NLP, the most important aspect of a strategy is considered to be the specific sequence of representational systems used to carry out the specific steps.

SURFACE STRUCTURE - The words or linguistic representations used to describe or stand for the actual primary sensory representations stored in the brain.

SYNESTHESIA - The process of overlap between representational systems, characterized by phenomena like "see-feel circuits," in which a person derives feelings from what he sees, and "hear-feel circuits," in which a person gets feelings from what he hears. Any two sensory modalities may be linked together.

TOTE - Developed by Miller, Galanter and Pribram (1960), the term stands for the sequence Test-Operate-Test-Exit, which describes the basic feedback loop used to guide all behavior.

TRANSDERIVATIONAL SEARCH - The process of searching back through one's stored memories and mental representations to find the reference experience from which a current behavior or response was derived.

TRANSLATING - The process of rephrasing words from one type of representational system predicates to another.

UTILIZATION - A technique in which a specific strategy sequence or pattern of behavior is paced or matched in order to leverage or influence another's response.

VISUAL - Relating to sight or the sense of sight.

www.ingramcontent.com/pod-product-compliance
Lightning Source LLC
Chambersburg PA
CBHW071558080526
44588CB00010B/951